The Church of England's Wish for the Restoring of Primitive Discipline
of Primitive Discipline
by John Gilbert

THE
Church of *England's*
W I S H
For the Restoring of
Primitive Discipline.

THE

Church of *England's*

WISH

For the Restoring of

Primitive Discipline;

Confidered, in Order to its being brought to Effect.

On which Occafion is fhewn the Inftitution, Nature, End, and Neceffity of Difcipline in the Church of Chrift.

To Debate of Ceremonies *and* Words in the Service, *&c. Not confidering the* power of the Keys, *upon which the Church is Founded, and the Reftoring of the Same; is to neglect a Confumption at the Heart, pretending only to Cure the Hair or the Nails.* H. Thorndike's Juft Weights and Meafures, *Page* 255.

LONDON:

Printed for W. Rogers, at the *Sun* againft St. *Dunftan's* Church in *Fleetftreet*. 1703.

PREFACE.

THE Repeated Assurances which our Gracious Queen has been pleased to give of her Purpose to Preserve the Church of England, and her known Zeal for the same; as also the Zealous Affection to the Church Expressed by both Houses of Parliament in their late Addresses, having given a just ground for those Hopes conceived and declared by the Convocation, That whatever may be wanting to restore our Church to its due Rights and Privileges, Her Majesty will have the Glory of doing it; And the Queen likewise having been Graciously Pleased, not only to approve, but assure their Confidence to this purpose, by her Answer, " That " she will always endeavour to Preserve " this Church in its Doctrine and Dis- " cipline: Why should not this be looked on as the proper time given this Church by the Providence of God to seek the being

A 3   restored

The Preface.

restored to the Authority given it by Christ Jesus; that the Primitive Discipline of Christ's Church may be Revived and Established with Effect in this our Church, for the good of Souls, and the intrest of our common Christianity? Yea, why may it not be Hoped, that at this juncture, (if the Pastors of the Church, who stand charged with the Ministry, shall Assert (as in Duty they ought) the Right of the Church to an Authority that may Oblige the Conscience, and Bind its Members to a Submission to this Discipline; and shall make it appear also that themselves, who have the care thereof committed to them on behalf of the Church, are desirous to discharge a Conscience in its Execution) the Civil Authority may lend an Assistance, the general good Will of Christians also concurring, to bring it to Effect? It is out of this hope, how faint soever, that the Author of this Tract has attempted to shew therein, That this Church has a Right to have her Discipline Restored, which it has in vain Wished to see effected from the beginning of the Reformation; That those who stand Trusted with this Ministry, cannot discharge a Conscience to God or his Church, but by doing their utmost towards it.

That

The Preface.

That it will not be a sufficient Excuse for such, at the day of Account to say, The Discipline of the Church has been lost, or the Corrupt Age would not endure it, unless their Conscience can Attest that they have been the more Zealous in their Endeavours to Retrieve it, as the necessary Remedy for Cure of that Corruption; that they have done what in them lies also to recover to the Church that Authority which Christ left it Invested with, for the Maintenance of Christianity: That the same Reasons which oblige all that desire to Profess Christianity, to become Members of the Church, ought to prevail with them to yield Effect to this Ministry, which is of God's providing, as the Means of obliging Christians to live up to the excellent Rules of their Holy Profession: That whatever Civil Power, being Christian, in that respect, thinks it self obliged to Maintain the Church, cannot want Evidence of its Obligation to give Effect and Force to this Discipline of the Church, which Carnal Christians are not likely to Submit to otherwise: The very Being of a Church importing this, That there be a Power and Authority, acknowledged for the Maintaining that Christianity which the Church, as a Society, stands Charged to Maintain, as

the

The Preface.

the Nature of all Societies must Impart a Power to Maintain themselves according to the Design and Rules of their Constitution.

Let me not be thought not to foresee many Censures, and much Opposition in this Attempt, which nevertheless the Part which I have in the Church's Ministry will oblige me to abide. I must expect it to be Objected by some, that there is no such thing as an Authority of such in Nature as the Discipline pretended to importeth, of Right belonging to the Church; that indeed there is no such thing as a Church endued with a Power to such Effect by the Ordinance of our Lord, or the Institution of his Apostles. But I take the Proof made in the following Treatise, That Discipline was of Apostolical Practice, to have obviated all that can be with any Force Objected against the Constitution of the Church, or its Right in this Particular: Inasmuch as Discipline implies the Church to be Constituted a Society, as the Ancient Practice of this Discipline Recorded in the Scripture implies also its Original to be from Christ and his Apostles. I must look that it will be Objected, notwithstanding. That the Ancient Discipline came to Effect by the voluntary Consent of Christians, that in times

of

The Preface.

of Persecution Submitted to such Rules as seemed necessary in that State of Things; and that now, all the Authority the Church hath is from the Laws of the Land in every Christian State; so that what Changes or Alterations are made by the Civil Power, shall take Place, in Bar to any Laws or Customs of the Church. But I am mistaken if any great matter can be made of this Objection. 'Tis true indeed, The Ancient Discipline came to Effect by the voluntary Consent of Christians; and the Church being a mere Spiritual Society, without any Temporal Power, to enforce by way of Constraint the Effect of its Ministry, it could not be otherwise. But though the Church could lay no outward Constraint, it nevertheless laid a Constraint upon the Conscience, so that those who Consented to submit unto its Discipline, could not have been Christians, had they not so consented. There was therefore an Authority Obliging them in Conscience to yield Effect to those Ministries which God had provided for the Maintenance and Propagation of Christianity. So that that voluntary Act was nevertheless a Duty, in respect of an Authority in the Church Claiming from them a Submission to its Discipline, though not constraining it by any External Force. Now
this

The Preface.

this being the Case, 'tis visible that the Church had an Authority from the Beginning, though this not a Temporal, but Spiritual Authority. It will therefore concern such as will have it, that the Civil Authority may make Changes or Alterations at its pleasure in the Laws and Customs of the Church, and that the Church has now no Authority, to shew by what Right any Civil Power, Professing Christianity, may defeat the Church of any part of the Right whereof it stands Possessed by the Original Institution of our Lord and his Apostles; or give a Reason at least, why the Authority of the Church, which being derived from Christ and his Apostles stood good against the Heathen Powers, should not stand good where the Civil Power Professeth Christianity, which will not be easily done. Whereas it is a very easie matter for me to shew on the contrary, That a State Professing Christianity, and the Protection thereof, ought not only to acknowledge the Authority which the Church has from Christ and the Apostles, but to imploy also its own Authority to render the other Effectual with such as being Christians more out of Intrest than Conscience would not submit otherwise to the Authority and Discipline of the Church.

Some

The Preface.

Some no doubt will say, 'tis Popery, or something like it, to revive Penances, Confession and Discipline. But in this Case I should not be afraid of either Reproach or Censure (were the Discipline of Penance free from Abuses in the Romish Church, and Executed to the Purposes of its Institution in the Church of Christ, that is to say, the Cure of Sin, and procuring in Penitents the disposition, that according to the Gospel qualifieth for Remission of Sins) freely to profess that I wished the Restoring of such Ecclesiastical Laws as might Restore the Church's Authority, to bring Sinners under the Discipline of Penance, though those Laws were such as the Church of Rome hath, and our Reformation hath not. Yet shall I have no Thanks on that side, when I have said, That the Church of Rome abuseth the Discipline of the Church, and the Penances it enjoyns to Ends not Warranted from Christianity, neglecting that upon which they take place in it. For the Discipline of Penance of Right is this, When any have visibly Transgressed that Profession upon which they were Admitted Members of the Christian Church by Baptism, to call such to an Account, and to enjoyn them such Acts of Humiliation and Self denial as may be instrumental

(the

The Preface.

(the Grace of God assisting) to work in them a True Repentance; and to Exclude them in part, or altogether from the Communion of the Church, till they shall have Submitted to such Acts of Penance as may warrant the Church to Admit them to her Communion again, as giving some assurance of their true Repentance, and presumption of their recovery of the State of Grace which alone entitles to it. But now this Discipline as Exercised, in the Church of Rome, how much soever it be pretended to the advantage of Christianity, is so perverted as rather to give encouragement to Sin. For whereas the Penitential Works should, according to the Practice of the Primitive Church be first enjoyned the Sinner, to work in him a true Humiliation, that thereby being in some measure satisfied of his true Repentance, the Church might with Authority Pronounce him Absolved from those Sins, which might be presumed throughly Repented of: In the Church of Rome the Absolution is first granted, and warranted upon the bare Confession to the Priest, and the Penitential Works that are afterwards imposed, not enjoyned with any Instructions of their being designed to work the Heart to Repentance, and effect the Change in it which

that

The Preface.

*that supposeth; but Deposed with intent
to appease and Satisfy the Divine Justice,
in reference to Punishments which this
may inflict notwithstanding the Remission
of the Sin. Wherein, as that Church acts
without Authority in Warranting the Pardon of Sin by giving Absolution before
it has procured the only Condition qualifying for it according to the Gospel Repentance: So instead of being Ministerial
as it ought to procure that Condition, it
sets it aside, or at least, gives advantage
to Men of Corrupt Hearts to set it aside,
and think themselves little concerned to
work their Hearts to a Repentance for
their Sins, or indeed to perform their Penances enjoyned to the forementioned mistaken purpose, when they are before rendred
secure as to the Pardon of their Sins, and
the Remission of all Punishment but what is
Temporal. There is yet a greater Evil in
the Doctrine of the Church of Rome relating to Penance, in what it teacheth, as
to the Vertue of the Priest's Absolution, that
this supplies the defects of a Man's Repentance, so that there is no absolute necessity
of Contrition, which is the sorrow to Repentance, according to the Gospel qualifying for Remission of Sins; but Attrition,
which is short of the other, being only the*
Sorrow

The Preface.

Sorrow that ariseth from fear of Punishment shall become sufficient by the Means of the Priest's Absolution. The Words of their Catechism Relating to this Matter are Cat. Trid. de Confes. Sac. &c. *these.* " Although it must be Confessed,
" that our Sins are Blotted out by Contri-
" tion, yet inasmuch as few arrive to so
" great a degree of Sorrow for them as that
" requires, they are therefore very few
" that can place their hope of Salvation
" in that way: Wherefore it was necessary
" that our most Merciful Lord should pro-
" vide for the Common Salvation of Man-
" kind by an Easier way, which out of his
" Wise Counsel he did, when he delivered
" the Keys of his Heavenly Kingdom to his
" Church. For according to the Doctrine
" of the Catholick Faith, it must be Be-
" lieved, and constantly Affirmed by all,
" that if a Man be but so Affected in his
" Mind, as to be sorry for the Sins he
" has committed, intending withal not
" to Sin for the time to come, although
" he have not that Sorrow which is suf-
" ficient to obtain Forgiveness, yet when
" he shall have duly Confessed his Sins
" unto the Priest, all his Sins shall be
" Forgiven and Remitted to him by the
" Power of the Keys. And even the
Concil Trid. Sess. 14.Cap. 4. Council of Trent it self allows that which

is

is not perfect Contrition to qualify for God's Grace and Pardon. Which Pretence of the Church of Rome, to supply the Defects of Mens Repentance, and abuse of that Condition which the Gospel requires to the Remission of Sins, as it is altogether without Warrant from Christ, so does it frustrate the Effect of its own Ministry, insomuch that it is rather Prejudicial than Ministerial to the Ends of Christianity. The Indulgencies likewise granted in the Church of Rome, are no other than abuses of the Power and Authority of the Church in Reference to Relaxations of Penance, which had place in the Primitive times in extraordinary cases, where Penitents shewed a more than ordinary Zeal in the Works of Humiliation they were appointed to undergo, or by some Eminent Acts of Piety shewed themselves to have throughly Repented them of their Sins, and that the Love of God had taken place in their hearts. In such cases many times Penitents were Admitted to the Communion of the Church before their performance of all the Penitential Acts that had been enjoyned them, the Cure of Sin appearing to be wrought in them which the Discipline of the Church intended. But this Practice can never warrant the Romish Indulgences, dispensed in favour

vour

The Preface.

vour of Penitents promiscuously, and without regard to Evidence of their Repentance; Not to mention the Unlawful Gain made by the Markets of them, and their use to other purposes than the Abatement, or Remission of Ecclesiastical Discipline, whilst it is pretended that there is a Stock of Merits in the Church, which are allowed to the Account of those to whom it grants these Indulgences. By this it may be discerned, that the Practice of Penance in the Church of Rome is quite different from what it of right ought to be in the Church of Christ: So that indeed that Church has little cause to Boast of her Discipline, unless it were used to better purposes, and made serviceable to the Ends of Christianity. Nevertheless I must say on the other side, that the Reformation which concerned it self justly in the removal of those abuses, should have been no less concerned to preserve a Discipline free from abuses in the Authority it ought to have in the Church of Christ. And this is what our first Reformers would have done, had not the abuses of Discipline been so great and vile, as to give advantage to a Corrupt Age, to despise and reject the Authority that should have given Effect thereto, on pretence of the Abuses therein. This then rendred their Attempt to Establish

Primitive

The Preface.

Primitive Discipline impracticable: But we, by Experience have seen and felt what they feared, namely, the Decay of Christian Piety from the loss of this Discipline, and are therefore the more concerned to do what is possible to be done towards the Restoring it, yet with this Care and Caution, that the Abuses be not Restored with it, yea, that they be effectually prevented for the future.

But others probably will censure my Zeal for Discipline, to betray an Affection to the Presbyterian Model. To such, my Answer and Defence is this, If any Sectaries whatever insist Zealously for that which deserves to be insisted on with Zeal by all good Christians; I shall not think shame to be Zealous for the same thing : So likewise if any of our Sects blame us for what is blame-worthy, I cannot think it justifiable in us to cast off the consideration of it, because they may have unduly Separated from the Church on pretence thereof. For Instance, If a Puritan blame us for this, that Scandalous and Profane Persons are not Censured as they ought to be, and Notorious Evil Livers Admitted to the Communion, whom we ought to keep from it : I will not allow indeed this to be a reasonable or just pretence for any to withdraw from

the

The Preface.

the Communion of the Church upon it: There being no manner of Reason to think that another's Wickedness should void the Effect or Benefit of the Sacrament to him that Worthily partakes of it. And besides, all Order and Government in the Church will fall to nothing, if every private Person may take upon him to Judge and Censure others, or make a Separation from, or cause Division in the Church for every Imperfection, or indeed, Abuse of the Church's Authority, or Neglect of them that are concerned to put its Discipline in Execution. But far be it from me to say or think that there is not great blame lying on us, and that justly, for the utter neglect of that Order which our Church hath taken in the Rubrick before the Communion, That if any, of those who intend to Communicate be an Open Notorious Evil Liver——" The Curate
" shall advertise him, in any wise not to
" presume to the Lord's Table till he have
" openly declared himself to have truly Re-
" pented and Amended his former Naughty
" Life, &c.—- And the same Order shall the
" Curate use with whom he perceiveth Ma-
" lice and Hatred to Reign, not suffering
" them to be partakers of the Lord's Table,
" until he knows them to be Reconciled: And
" if one of the Parties so at Variance be con-
" tent

"tent to forgive the other from the bottom
"of the heart--and to make amends for that
"he himself hath Offended, and the other
"Party will not be perswaded to a godly Uni-
"ty,--the Minister in that case ought to Ad-
"mit the Penitent Person to the Holy Com-
"munion, and not him that is Obstinate.
Which Order of the Rubrick seems to be
made in Pursuance of the 26th. Canon, the
Title of which is, Notorious Offenders
not to be Admitted to the Communion,
and to bring to Effect that Rule which pro-
vides thus. "No Minister shall in any
"wise Admit to the Receiving of the Holy
"Communion, any of his Cure or Flock,
"which be openly known to live in Sin No-
"torious without Repentance, nor Malici-
"ous Persons not Reconciled,&c. Doubtless
those that have the Cure of Souls among us
(whose Concern it is to see these good Orders of the Church of England take place)
are not the less, but rather the more concerned to consider of means that may bring
these Orders of our Church to some Effect;
for that our neglect herein is made a pretence by some of our Adversaries, to justifie their Unreasonable Separation: For tho'
the Pretence be such as cannot be justly insisted on by them, yet does it lay to the
charge of those that have the Cure of Souls

The Preface.

in the Church a Neglect, which I am to seek how they will be able to answer to God or his Church, or even to any good Christian, taking Offence thereat. Thus in another like Instance suppose a Puritan to find fault, that in the Office of Burial we express an Hope touching the Resurrection of the Person Deceased, to Eternal Life, which is so far from being sure and certain as we term it, with reference to all we bury promiscuously, that indeed it is unwarrantable, and ought not to be in the least mentioned, with reference to many, whose Lives have been known to be notoriously Vitious and Wicked, and of whose Repentance there appears little presumption (the Church especially being concerned that no hope nor encouragement be given to wicked Livers, who will be apt enough to encourage themselves in wickedness from the least Countenance the Church shall give to such as may have reconciled their hopes of Heaven with the enjoyment of their Lusts.) I cannot say that this is no Objection, but, that it would be none if the Discipline of the Church took place, to cut off from the Body of the Church all notoriously Vicious and Wicked Livers; For the Order of the Church for Burial of the Dead, appointing that the Office be not used for any that die Unbaptized

zed or Excommunicate, *it might be presumed of all Admitted into the Church
by Baptism and dying in its Communion, that
having lived according to their Christian
Profession (which supposing them not to
have done, and the Discipline of the Church
taking place they must have been Excluded
that Communion) they were in a state of
Salvation at their Death; concerning whom
therefore, as we should not be* without hope,
*so we should not be afraid to express that
Hope, even in Terms expressing a Confidence
and Assurance in God and Christ for their
having a part in the Resurrection of the
Just.*

*And now as for the Reasons given in these
Instances, somewhat relating to the Matter
in hand, I cannot think it justifiable in us,
if any Sectaries blame us for what is
blame-worthy, to lay aside the Consideration of
what in Duty ought to be done, to redress
whatever may be amiss. So in like manner,
I cannot think the Concern, which with all
good Christians we ought to have for the
Discipline of Christ's Church, should be laid
aside, because some of our Sectaries have
appeared seemingly more zealous for it than
we, or have charged us wrongfully with a
want of Zeal in this Case, or made it a Pretence of Separation to set up a better Discipline. On the contrary this should encrease*

our

our zeal to Establish, if possible, the True Primitive Discipline, and bring it to Effect in the Church, to take off thereby all blame from our selves, and all occasion from the Adversary. But at the same time that I have said this, being willing to do our Presbyterians Right so far as they assert Christ *the* Head of the Church, *to have therein appointed a Government in the hands of* Church Ministers *distinct from the* Civil Magistrate, *and to have committed to these the* Keys of the Kingdom of Heaven, *by vertue whereof they have* Power to Remit and Retain Sins, *to shut that Kingdom against the impenitent, and to open it unto Penitent Sinners; and that therefore this Power ought to be Exercised, and a Discipline kept up in the Church of Christ; I must declare them nevertheless very much in the wrong, as they seek to have the Government of the Church in their* Presbyteries, *Excluding* Bishops, *and denying their Ancient Right, (whereas there is Evidence beyond Contradiction, that for many Ages the Rule and Government of the Church was managed by Bishops in Conjunction with their Presbyters; the Bishop in every particular Church having the Government in Chief, his Presbyters having part with him as Assistants, joyned to, and with him in the Work, yet so as themselves were subjected also to his*

Auto-

The Preface.

Authority, to be kept thereby under the Rules of Discipline). I must also declare that the Schism, they have made in the Church, upon this and other undue, and unwarrantable grounds, has brought on this Evil Consequence among many others, That the Discipline of the Church they pretend to be so zealous for, is by this very means less practicable and less effectual than otherwise it would or might be made to be. For the Unity of the Church is that which gives Strength to its Authority, and Effect to its Discipline. If Men were under no Obligations from their Christianity to be Members of the Church, the Authority that Admits them to, or Excludes them from it, would in no respect bind the Conscience. And if a number of Christians agreeing together can make themselves a Church, and have the Sacraments among them to the same Effect as they are had in the Church; they then are under no concern to Obey them that have the Rule over them, or to regard their Censures or any of their Attempts to bring them under Discipline. 'Tis a much like Case, as the Church now stands Divided by Schism; suppose its Discipline employed to bring a notorious wicked Liver to Penance, suppose him kept back from the Sacrament, or Excommunicate untill he shall Repent, and give Evidence of his Repent-

a 4   *ance;*

The Preface.

...... the Church's Censure in ...., shall have but little Effect, .. long .. the Offender can join himself to another Society of Christians, and be allowed among them the hopes of Salvation, and the means thereof, which his own Church had denied him. This I look upon as the cause, in part, why Discipline in the Church of England has been so much neglected; it being looked on as of little or no avail, as the Church is divided into so many several Sects, which gives opportunity to Offenders to stand it out with the Church, or to go off to another Communion. Not but that I think it a very weak thing in Pastors to neglect their Duty in this particular, for fear of such an event. The Primitive Church might as well have been deterred from its Discipline for fear of Mens turning Heathens. But this the Church feared not, it being at the hazard of their Souls if they despised the Church and her Power or departed from it; and 'tis at the same hazard if Men despise it, and join with Schismaticks. Nevertheless, as all men are not sensible of the Danger, nor likely to become sensible of it, whilst Christians keep up Separate Communions; it should give Occasion one would think, to those that are zealous for the Establishment of a Discipline in the Church, to bethink themselves first, how the Union of the Church may

may be restored, which would make its Dis-cipline effectual indeed, to the true ends and purposes of its appointment and institution in the Church of Christ.

I would if possible, obviate all Prejudices, and therefore desire to be believed, when I profess my self to have no other Design in what I have done to remonstrate the useful-ness and necessity of Discipline, than the common good of Christianity and God's Church, and my own particular good so far only as my Soul may have benefit from the discharge of my Duty, and in, and by the the Establishment of this Discipline it self. And Charity cannot impute to me any other design, it being evident that I may expect no thanks from any of the Parties into which the Christian Church is now unhappily divided. From the Papists I shall have none, having said in effect, that they pretend to Discipline, but use it not aright, yea, per-vert it, even to the Prejudice of Christia-nity: From our Dissenters I can expect none, having said, that they to little purpose are zealous for a Discipline in the Church, when as their Schism has rendred it for the most part ineffectual. If I might expect any thanks, I would hope for it from those of our own Communion ; yet can it be from few of these. For this Plea for Discipline suppo-seth that we have it not, or at least, not to

the

the purpose we ought to have it, and implies a fault somewhere, that we have it not, or at least not to purpose. Besides, Discipline strikes at Men's Sins, the Talk of it therefore gives Disturbance, and an endeavour to set it up is an Offence like that of plucking away the Pillows from under the Elbows of such as desire to sleep at their ease.

I shall not be surprized therefore, if many among our selves shew themselves uneasie, and Censure my Labour in this as a design to advance the Power of Church-men. I shall freely own the Clergy to be Parties in this Case, as they have a part in this Ministry from Christ Jesus, therefore they must needs be Parties; but at the same time they are obliged to challenge their Right in this, as in other parts of their Ministry at their utmost hazard, and may therefore with as much reason be suspected to seek themselves, or Power and Authority to themselves in any, or all other parts of their Ministry as in this, and consequently laid aside in all their Ministry as in this part of it: Which if allowed them, does only, together with the Power bring on them a greater Charge; a Charge so great, in respect of the Trust lying upon them, to Rule well the Church of God, that 'tis to be feared, many of the Clergy themselves could be well contented to be without the Power, not

to

The Preface.

to have the Duty, nor the neglect thereof to lie upon them, or be Charged to their Account. If the Discipline of the Church were once Restored, the Care of Governing well the Church of God (which by this must come on the Bishops of the Church, and which will not only lie upon them, but they also will be constrained to take upon them and to discharge) will be so great, that he that discharges well and faithfully the Duty will never be envied the advantages of the Office, not at least by Men of Conscience, who must look upon themselves bound to undergo the Labours, Difficulties, and Hazards of the one, if they take upon them the other. The Parochial Minister also will find himself obliged to a more laborious work than that of Preaching to his Congregation every Lord's Day; it will lie upon him to inspect the Lives of his whole Flock, to Visit Families, to Labour in Exhortations, Warnings, Reconciliations, and several other Cares of a Faithful Pastor; and to fulfil the Work of his Ministry, in those things there will appear a necessity that he approve himself in much Patience, in Meekness, in Charity, in Labours, in Diligence, in Watchings, in Self-denial, by Honour and Dishonour, by Evil Report and Good Report, as Proud, yet not abusing his Power in the Ministry, as Weak, or as a Fool, yet

Knowing,

The Preface.

Knowing, and not afraid to use the Authority he has as God's Minister; to Admonish, to Reprove, to Rebuke them that Sin, that others may fear. And who is sufficient for these things? that he should desire an Authority of this kind, if this were not a part of the Ministry that he stands entrusted with by God for the good of Souls, of which he must give Account. Besides, the Clergy themselves must become subject to this Discipline, if Restored; and if it be Exercised according to Ancient Practice, it will be more severe upon them than others, and call them to account for failures in reference to their Office as well as irregularities in their Manners. It must therefore be a very weak, as well as groundless suspition, that shall charge the Clergy with Self-seeking or Pride in their desire of Discipline. My fear and suspition is of another Nature, viz. that many of them may think it is better with them as it is (they now living at ease, freed of the Care, and Burden, and Hazard that would attend the impartial Exercise and Execution of the Primitive Discipline, their own necks also got from under the Yoke) and so content themselves to let go the Discipline of the Church altogether upon the Common Excuse, That the Corrupt Age will not endure it. But such as are enclinable to think thus, that

things

things are best as they are, and can be content after this manner, let them impartially search and examine their own hearts whether there lie no Corruption there that makes them not to love this Discipline, and bethink themselves whether the Excuse upon which we are apt to hold our selves Excusable, giving and taking it as an Excuse to and from each other, will stand in any stead at the day of Account. No! the very Excuse will rise up in the Judgment, and Condemn such as are content to have the Discipline of Christ's Church laid aside in a time when there is the most need of it, to Reform that Corruption that Exalts it self against it. But I go farther than need is; I am not to think that any of my Brethren in the Ministry will weaken my hands, but rather strengthen them.

I am not under any Apprehension therefore of meeting in my way, what would be an invidious charge, That I step before my Superiors in this Work. I plead indeed the necessity of Discipline, but pretend not to give Rules for it, nor yet to say how far the Present times are capable of those which were Rules in the Primitive Church, which should therefore be at least in some measure regarded by the present Church, if it would be one and the same with that which was from the Beginning, nor
indeed

Indeed do I take upon me so much as to propose the ways and means by which the Restoration of Discipline is to be attempted: I look on these as belonging to Superiors, who are obliged to answer and account for what ought to be done therein. Yea, with them I leave, and to them submit the Opinion which I have thought my self obliged to offer in this matter. I leave it with them, because if there be Truth in what I urged for the necessity of Discipline, it will be their Concern, and ought to be their Care to bring it to some Effect. I submit it to them to avoid the Offence which might be otherwise given by speaking and insisting upon Truth out of due Time. For I am sensible that Unity in the Church is of so great Advantage to the Service of God and our Common Christianity, that it ought to cover not only very great Imperfections in the Laws of the Church, but even many faults in the Administration of those Laws. Nevertheless, as in this Case the Church of England hath her self declared the Imperfection, I am satisfied that I give no just cause of Offence in declaring what is wanting: And as things are come to that pass, that instead of faults in the Administration of Discipline according to imperfect Rules, we have now in a manner, no Administration of it at all, it seems time to say what ought to be the

Disci-

The Preface.

Discipline of Christ's Church, and to Charge home the Neglect of the Administration of what is, wheresoever the fault lies: Provided it be with deference and submission to Superiors, that they be allowed their Right to judge whether the Time be proper and safe to make an Attempt towards the regaining this Discipline to the Church, (I mean safe in reference to the Intrest of God's Church and the Unity thereof, not in reference to the Worldly Intrest of the Persons concerned to act for the Church at their utmost Peril and Hazard in every proper and needful Time) as also what means are to be used, as well for procuring the Establishment thereof, as for the rendring it Effectual when Establish'd.

The only Offence that I need fear my self to have given is in this, That I have undertaken a Design of this Consequence and am not able to go through with it as it deserves; which may indeed give Offence to Good Men, and which is worse, be a Prejudice to the Rights of God's Church: But I think this, That no Instrument is insufficient in the hands of God, who often chooses the Meanest, that it may appear to be his Work, and that the Praise may be to God and not to Man; And if the Thing be from him that I stand up for, he will stay up the Feeble and Heavy Hands that are held up for the
Truth,

The Preface.

Truth, even till it shall have prevailed. I likewise think that there are many good Men (Zealous for the Cause of God and his Church) ready at hand to strengthen that which in me is weak; and that such will excuse my weakness on the score of my having appeared forward to do to the utmost of my Ability.

THE

THE
Church of *England's*
WISH,

In Reference to the Restoring of Primitive Discipline, &c.

CHAP. I.

THE *Church* of *England* (as it's well known) in the *Commination against Sinners*, hath declared a great Zeal for the renewing of that *Ancient Discipline* of Penance which was in Force in the Primitive Church. Its Words are these : " Brethren, In the Pri-
" mitive Church there was a Godly Disci-
" pline, that at the beginning of *Lent*;
" such Persons as stood convicted of noto-
" rious Sin, were put to open Penance,

B " and

" and punished in this World, that their
" Souls might be saved in the Day of the
" Lord; and that others admonish'd by
" their Example, might be the more afraid
" to offend.   Instead whereof, (until the
" said *Discipline* may be *restored* again,
" which is *much to be wished*) it is thought
" good, *&c.*   Concerning which Discipline, in one of the *Homilies* it saith thus.

Homily of
the *Right*
Use of the
Church.
Part 2. " In the *Primitive Church*, which was
" most *holy* and *godly*, and in the which *due*
" *Discipline* with Severity, was used against
" the Wicked, open Offenders were not
" suffered once to enter into the House of
" the Lord, nor admitted to Common-
" Prayer, and the use of the Holy Sacra-
" ments, with other true Christians, until
" they had done open Penance before the
" whole Church.   And this was practised
" not only upon mean Persons, but upon
" the Rich, Noble, and Mighty Persons,
" yea, upon *Theodosius;* that puissant and
" mighty Emperor; whom for committing
" a grievous and wilful Murder, St. *Am-*
" *brose* Bishop of *Milain* reproved sharply,
" and did also *Excommunicate* the said Em-
" peror, and brought him to open Penance.
" And they that were so justly exempted
" and banished (as it were) from the
" House of the Lord, were taken, as they
" be indeed, for Men divided and separa-
                                        " ted

"ted from Chrift's Church, and in moft
"dangerous Eftate, yea, as St. *Paul* faith,
"even *given unto Satan* the Devil for a
"time, and their Company was fhunned
"and avoided of all Godly Men and Wo-
"men, until fuch time as they by Repen-
"tance and Publick Penance were recon-
"ciled. Thus was the Practice, as it
faith afterwards, *When Religion was moft*
Pure, and nothing fo Corrupt as it hath been
of late days. Comparing this in the *Homi-*
ly with that Paffage in the *Commination*
againft Sinners, there is Reafon to conclude, That the Church apprehended
Difcipline to be of *Primitive Practice*, ufed
in the *Pureft Times* of Chriftianity; to be
likewife neceffary and ufeful for the Good
of Souls, for the well Government of
Chriftians in Godlinefs, and for reducing
Sinners to the Way of Righteoufnefs; and
that this was the true Ground of the Defire expreffed for its being reftored. This
the *Expedient* devifed and ufed by the
Church in its ftead, until that may be effected, does alfo plainly fhew. For to
what End ferveth the *Commination againft*
Sinners, but by Threats of God's Judgments (which 'tis a vain thing for any
guilty Soul not to think, or not to acknowledge due to its Sins) to awaken
Men to do of themfelves that which the

Difci-

The Church of England's Wish.

Discipline of the Church (were it in Force) would call on and constrain them to do? Namely, To repent them of their Sins, and amend their Doings, and make their Lives to answer their Holy Profession for the future; thereby to regain the Hope of God's Favour, and an Interest in his Mercy, forfeited by their Transgressions. And the Appointment of this, till the other might be restored, intimates that could it be restored, it would be of greater Efficacy for this purpose, than this *Commination* can be thought to be.

This appearing, it ought surely to be taken into Consideration, Whether those who are intrusted on behalf of the Church, to execute its Ministry for the Good of Souls and the Interest of Christianity, do enough towards the discharge of a good Conscience, in *wishing* once a Year, at reading the *Office* on *Ashwednesday*, that the *Discipline* of the Church were *restored*. Or whether it lye not upon them to do something towards the *regaining* of it, that the Church may be restored to the Power it hath from Christ, and that Power employed to the Effect intended by our Blessed Lord, who committed the same to his Church. If any, when this comes to be considered, can content themselves only to *wish* the *Discipline* of the Church *restored*,

red, without moving either Hand or Foot towards it ; they are such as either understand not the Usefulness of the Discipline of the Church to Christian Purposes, or make no Conscience of discharging a Duty to God in the Execution of its Ministry to serve those *Ends.* I say this, because an honest Conscience can never satisfy it self, that *wishing* the Ministry of the Church to take place, and have the Effect it ought to have, is the same with *doing* that which may restore and render it effectual. Wishes are indeed Marks of a good Intention, and an acceptable Zeal, where no more is possible to be done ; but ever to wish, and make no Attempt towards the Thing wished for, if it be Zeal, is such as is a Reproach to it self. Suppose then only for the present, what in this Treatise is to be proved and made appear, That *Discipline* is of the Appointment of *Christ* and his *Apostles,* and a *Ministry* with which the Church stands charged at all times, as being *absolutely necessary* for its good Government ; and shall not *Pastors* stand convict hereby, that they can never discharge the Trust upon their hands to God and his Church, nor be *True* to their *Master,* or to the *Souls* which are their Care, unless they do their utmost towards the restoring and executing the Discipline of

B 3

Christ's

Chrift's Church? Shall not even *Private Chriftians* hereby ftand convinced, that whilft the Church is without its Difcipline, they are without the Benefit of it to their Souls ; and be hence concerned, not only to wifh but to do what on their parts may be done, to reftore that Difcipline, which being reftored, may be minifterial to the good of their own Souls in particular, as well as ferviceable to the general good of God's Church? The Duty of many, and the Concerns of all Chriftians in this matter, will appear, I am perfuaded, more plain than to be difowned, and of more Importance than to be thought fit to be laid afide, if there be Evidence found to prove, (what I have defired leave to fuppofe only for the prefent, but taking it upon me to make the Proof,) That Difcipline hath its beginning from Chrift and his Apoftles : That thefe left in the Church a Power and Authority for exercifing and executing thereof : And that to the Authority of the Church for this purpofe, all Chriftians ought to be fubject.

Let us fee then what Proof may be made of this from Scripture, as alfo from the Practice of the Primitive Church : For I may challenge this, That where in Scripture a Foundation is laid for the Church's Practice, there the Practice of the Primitive

tive Church giveth Light to the true
Senſe of the Scripture relating to that
Matter.

CHAP. II.

NOW as to the Origine of Church
Diſcipline, I take upon me to prove
it a Divine Inſtitution, founded on the
Laws of Chriſt and his Apoſtles. Could
this indeed not be proved, yet ſuppoſing
it uſeful and beneficial, tending to the advancement of Godlineſs; as to all other
Bodies a Right is allowed to eſtabliſh Orders to regulate themſelves by, and a Power
of making Laws for the benefit and common good of their Society, and of excluding thoſe from their Body who will not
ſubmit to them; ſo ought the Church to
be allowed a Power to appoint a Diſcipline,
to which all her Members ſhould be ſubject; provided the Diſcipline be ſuch as is
not inconſiſtent with the Laws of the Goſpel, which is the Rule to which the Society of the Church in general is to be
ſubject: And much more is this to be allowed, if the Diſcipline in its due exerciſe
effectually miniſter to the very ſame Ends
of Piety and Virtue which the Laws of the

Go-

Gospel and the Christian Religion designed to promote. In this respect alone the Establishment of it would be lawful, and the Submission to it necessary. But this reacheth not the present Case ; which is not, Whether the Church may appoint a Discipline within it self, and its Members be bound to submit thereunto ; but, That the Church is obliged to restore that Discipline which anciently was, and all Christians concerned to give and yield thereto the effect it ought to have in the Church of Christ. Now nothing less than a Proof of its being of Divine Institution, can lay on the Church an Obligation to this purpose : For the Church having a Power of making Laws within it self, may indeed if it see fit, set up a Discipline on account of its Expediency and Usefulness to the Ends of Christianity : But its being expedient or useful to Ends of the Christian Religion, will not oblige the Church of necessity to set it up or to restore it ; the Church being Judge of the Expediency, and free to use any other Means that may be thought as effectually to serve those Ends. But if it appear that Discipline is a part of the Ministry with which Christ has charged his Church ; then shall the Church be obliged as to execute, so to hold, and keep, and maintain the same ; and private Christians

in

in Conscience as well as for Unity's sake to submit thereunto : Yea, the Church shall be obliged to restore it, if lost, as well as to reform Abuses in its Exercise; to assert the Powers it hath from Christ to execute this part of its Ministry, and its Right to that Power if she be despoiled of it, or if any Attempt be made to weaken her Authority, or to wrest it out of her hands.

And that Discipline is an Order Instituted by our Saviour and his Apostles, will appear plainly, after we shall have laid together what is to be found to this purpose in Scripture, and compare the same with the Proceedings in the Primitive Times of Christianity ; which we shall perceive consonant to the Rules of Christ and his Apostles in the Case, and declarative of the meaning of those Rules.

In the First place, I take notice of our Lord's giving the *Keys of the Kingdom of Heaven,* together with the Power of *remitting* and *retaining* Sins, to his Church. This we find given first to St. *Peter*, Matth. 16. 19. in these Words, " I will give un-
" to thee the Keys of the Kingdom of
" Heaven ; and whatsoever thou shalt
" bind on Earth, shall be bound in Hea-
" ven ; and whatsoever thou shalt loose on
" Earth, shall be loosed in Heaven. And
again,

again, *Matth.* 18. 17. to the Body of his Disciples; " If he will not hear thee, *&c.* " tell it to the Church ; but if he neglect " to hear the Church, let him be unto " thee as an Heathen and a Publican. Ve- " rily I say unto you, Whatsoever ye shall " bind on Earth, shall be bound in Hea- " ven; and whatsoever ye shall loose on " Earth, shall be loosed in Heaven. And again , *John* 20. 23. to his Twelve Apo- stles; " Whose soever Sins ye remit, they " are remitted unto them ; and whose " soever Sins ye retain, they are retained. 'Tis needless for me to go about to prove to Persons unprejudiced , That the Power given to St. *Peter,* and that given the rest of the Disciples, is one and the same. *Binding* and *loosing* are doubtless of the same Import with *remitting* and *retaining Sins* : And as this is the Effect of the Power of the Keys, it is to be supposed of them that are empower'd to work this Ef- fect, that they have the same Power given them, which the Keys of the Kingdom of Heaven import. And what that is, is the Enquiry that I am at present concerned with. Now the proper Use of a Key is to open a Door, to give entrance to those we think fit to admit, or to shut and lock it against such as we would exclude the House. According therefore to the most

natu-

natural, and least forced Sense of the Words, *the Keys of the Kingdom of Heaven* import a Power of admitting into the *House* or *Church* of God, or of shutting out and excluding thence; the Church of Christ being called the *Kingdom of Heaven*, as being the Society wherein God's Kingdom is set up, where the God of Heaven reigneth and ruleth, and where his Laws and Will are observed and obeyed from the Heart: Or, as the Admittance to that Society giveth Right to an Inheritance in God's Eternal Kingdom in Heaven; and the being excluded thence, importeth the being shut out of the Heavenly Kingdom, into which none have Right to enter, but those who are of the Family and Houshold, *i. e.* the Church of Christ: In this respect the Power of the Keys may imply the admitting to, or excluding from Heaven it self; though this, not in a strict Sense, but as the one ordinarily dependeth on the other, and as there is so far a Relation between them, that a due Admission into the Church of Christ, giveth ground to hope for an Admittance into his Heavenly Kingdom; as on the other hand, an Exclusion from his Church on Earth giveth cause to fear an Exclusion from his Kingdom in Heaven; and doth indeed exclude thence, without Repentance for those Sins which merit-

merited Exclufion from the Church, as having firft deferved Exclufion from Heaven. *Binding* and *loofing*, and *retaining* and *remitting* Sins, as I have faid, import the fame thing: For where there is no hope of Sins being forgiven, there Sin may be faid to remain, as it were, bound upon the Confcience, the Guilt taking hold of the Confcience in fuch manner, that it can no way get clear of it; where on the other hand there is hope of Forgivenefs, the Knot is loofed which bound Men over to Punifhment. Now thefe being faid to be Effects of the *Power of the Keys*, it is intimated that this Power opening and giving admittance into the Church of Chrift, and thereby to the hope of God's Pardon as to our Sins, and of admittance into his Heavenly Kingdom, does therein remit Mens Sins, and let them loofe from the Punifhment to which they were bound by them; as on the other hand, that it retaineth and bindeth them upon the Confcience, when it fhutteth out and excludeth from the Church of Chrift, thereby excluding and fhutting out from the hope of God's Promifes, whether as to Pardon or Salvation. Moreover, thofe Words of our Saviour, *Tell the Church*, and the Obligation prefumed on all to *hear the Church*, as to what it might admonifh them, about

their

their Faults complained of, and the confequence to thofe that fhall refufe to *hear the Church*, (to be looked on and accounted as an *Heathen* or a *Publican*,) and the Reafon immediately given upon it, in the words, *Verily I fay unto you, Whatfoever ye fhall bind on Earth, fhall be bound in Heaven ; and whatfoever ye fhall loofe on Earth, fhall be loofed in Heaven;* (wherein as it's implied that the *Church* proceed to *bind* or *loofe,* according as Men fhall hear or not hear what it fhall fay to them, in reference to what may have been done by them contrary to their Chriftian Duty, fo it is alfo declared that the Sentence of the Church on Earth fhall be ratified in Heaven.) Thefe together intimate plainly a Power lodged in the Church to take Cognizance of what Men may do contrary to their Duty, and a neceffity on them to fubmit to the Church's Authority, in what the Church fhall think fit to direct or admonifh them thereupon ; and that their Sins fhall be *bound upon them,* fo as not to be forgiven by God, if the Church fhall proceed to cenfure their Crimes, when it cannot prevail with them to amend.

It is not my purpofe to fay, that the Inferences I have made from thefe Scriptures, and the Reafons given for drawing thofe Inferences, and to argue the meaning

ing of them that which I have given, are
to be the Title upon which the Right of
the Church to this Power of the Keys,
and to a Discipline (being the effect of
this Power, limiting the Conditions, upon
compliance with which, Men may be admitted into the Church, and to the Privileges thereof ; but in case of Non-com-
pliance, excluded and shut out, as from
the Church, so from the Privileges and
Hopes belonging thereto) standeth or falleth. But that, these Scriptures well
bearing this Sense, and the Inferences easily deducible from them, the Practice of
the Apostles and the Primitive Church being such as would and must have been, had
the Authority and Power implied to be given in these Scriptures, been given in the
plainest Terms that could be expressed,
the subsequent Practice shall confirm this
to be the Sense of those Scriptures, which
has been said to be ; and these Scriptures
again shall be looked on as a good Foundation for that Power and Discipline
which the Church from the beginning exercised : And when it shall appear from
other Scriptures, that the Apostles in their
time took care for this Power and Discipline to be employed and executed; as it
shall be thought that these did this by Authority from their Great Master, so it shall
be

be an Obligation upon the Church to do the same at all times.

This Power of the Church therefore, and its Discipline, shall stand as on a firm Foundation, being built upon these Scriptures, notwithstanding another Sense may be given of them; inasmuch as they who may give to them another Sense, shall not be able to wrest them from this. Several I know, heretofore Adversaries to the Power and Authority of the Church, have endeavoured to give of these Scriptures a different meaning, and to wrest them from the Sense here supposed; but Answers having been given on behalf of the Church, that have silenced the Adversary, I do not think my self concerned to revive the Controversy. But a Person lately, concerned to uphold the Power and Authority of the Church, having nevertheless given up these Scriptures, as not belonging to, or at least as very improperly belonging to the Matter they have been here applied to; I think my self concerned to consider what is said thereupon. I mean what is said by the *Reverend Bishop* of *Sarum,* in his *Exposition* of the *Thirty nine Articles.* I must do Right to his Lordship in the first place, and say, That the most of what may be found in his Book to such purpose, is not urged against the due Pow-

er

er and Authority of the Church, but in opposition to the exorbitant Power and Authority claimed by the *Pope* and Church of *Rome.* Therefore it would not be a just suspicion, should it be thought design to undermine the Church in its Doctrine or Discipline, in a Book wherein much is said with great Learning for the Defence of both. But there being no necessity to deny these Scriptures to have their full force for establishing the Authority and Power of the Church, in defence of what *our Church* has acted in the *Reformation,* against the pretended Power and Authority of the *Pope* or *Church of Rome* ; and it seeming to me that his Lordship, by endeavouring to give another Meaning to these Scriptures, with purpose to overthrow an Authority that cannot stand upon them in their true Meaning, has thereby drawn away some of the chief Stones out of the Foundation upon which the due Power and Authority of the Church standeth ; by which the Building seems weakned, and the Discipline of the Church not to stand firm upon the Props with which his Lordship would uphold it : I therefore for that Reason only, shall debate the Sense of these Scriptures, that they properly belong to that which they have been here applied to. It is said then

in

in the Expofition, Pag. 199. in a Debate
about that Scripture. *I will give thee the*
Keys of the Kingdom of Heaven: that by the
Words *Kingdom of Heaven* " generally
" through the Gofpel, the Difpenfation of
" the Meffias is underftood; that there-
" fore the moft natural and leaft forced
" Expofition of the Words muft be, that
" St. *Peter* was to open the Difpenfation
" of the Gofpel. The proper ufe of a Key
" being to open a Door; that this agrees
" with the Words, *He that hath the Key of*
" *the Houfe of* David, and with the Phrafe
" of the *Key of Knowledge,* with which the
" Lawyers are defcribed. And that this
" agrees with what S. *Peter* did in opening
" the Gofpel to the *Jews,* and in opening the
" Door to the *Gentiles,* Preaching to *Corne-*
" *lius,* &c. That this is a clear and plain
" Senfe of the Words, and thofe who would
" carry them further, and underftand by
" the Kingdom of Heaven our Etertnal
" Happinefs muft ufe many diftinctions, *&c.*
After which are thefe Words. " Though at
" the fame time it is not to be denied but
" that under the Figure of Keys, the Power
" of Difcipline, and the Conduct and Ma-
" nagement of Chriftians *may be underftood.*
By which laft words you fee I am not to
conteft with the *Expofition* what is granted
in it, that under the Figure of Keys the

Mat. 16.
19.

Rev. 3. 7.
Luke 11.
52.

C   Power

Power of Difcipline may be underftood, and confequently this Scripture in fome fenfe may refer thereto ; but that it is properly applicable to this Matter. And to make this appear, I fay as the *Expofi-tion,* that by the Words *Kingdom of Hea-ven* generally through the Gofpel, the *dif-penfation of the Meffias* is underftood ; but then by the Difpenfation of the Meffias we are to underftand as well the whole Oeconomy, by which the Kingdom of the Meffias is Ordered and Governed, as alfo the Body of the Subjects of his King-dom, *i. e.* his Church, as the Preaching of his Gofpel for gathering a People to become Subjects in his Kingom. Thus in the Words of the Baptift and of our Sa-

Mat 3 2.   viour, cited in the *Expofition* ; *Repent, for the Kingdom of Heaven is at hand :* by the

Mark 1.   Kingdom of Heaven is meant a *New Oeco-*
15.   *nomy* different from that of *Mofes.* And again, *The Time is fulfilled, the Kingdom of God is at Hand* ; given for a Reafon why Men fhould Repent and Believe the Gofpel, for that the Time was now come, in the which God would Govern them by a New Oeconomy. Thus it alfo fignifies the Body of Chriftians, or the Church, in the following Paffages : " Whofoever fhall do

Mat. 5 19   " and teach them, the fame fhall be cal-
" led great in the *Kingdom of Heaven,* i. e.
among

" among Christians. And except your Righ-
" teousness exceed that of the Scribes and
" Pharisees, ye shall in no case enter into
" the Kingdom of Heaven, *i. e.* ye can-
" not be Christians. And again, *For of* Mark
" *such is the Kingdom of God, i. e.* of such 14, 15.
" Temper and Disposition are they who are
" the Church of God. And whosoever shall
" not receive the *Kingdom of God* as a lit-
" tle Child, he shall not enter *therein; i. e.*
whosoever shall not receive the Gospel or
Word of God with that Meekness and Sub-
missiveness and Humility as is in Children,
shall neither have entrance into his Kingdom of Grace here, nor of Glory hereafter; *i. e.* neither into his Church, nor into Heaven. And in the Parable where the
Kingdom of Heaven, i. e. the *Church,* is Com-
pared to a *Net full of Fishes of all sorts,*
good and bad. The Words *Kingdom of*
Heaven therefore signifying usually the
Church of Christ and the Government
thereof, (and the proper use of a Key being to open a Door, as the Exposition
saith rightly); the *Keys* of the Kingdom
of Heaven shall properly signify the Power or Authority of Admitting to, or Excluding from the Church, and the Discipline
Cond cting and Governing Christians within the same. And this shall best agree
with the Scripture from whence this Ex-

preſſion ſeems borrowed; namely that which was ſaid to *Eliakim* Son of *Hilkiah*, Eſai. 22. 23. And *the Key of the Houſe of* David *will I lay upon his Shoulder, ſo he ſhall open and none ſhall ſhut, and he ſhall ſhut and none ſhall open:* And with what is ſaid of our Lord's having the *Key of the Houſe of* David, *Rev.* 3. 7. When as *Eliakim* being ſet over the King's Court, and having the *Government* thereof *Committed into his Hand,* Ver. 21. is ſaid to have the *Key of the Houſe,* to Admit and Exclude whom he pleaſed; ſo the Apoſtles by having the *Keys of the Kingdom of Heaven,* ſhall be underſtood to be made under our Lord, Stewards of his Church, with Power of Admitting to, and Excluding from it by Baptiſm and Penance. And if it will be an Argument of any moment to make out the truth of the Interpretation, that there was an accompliſhment of the Thing in St. *Peter's* Perſon, to whom the Keys were firſt given; There are Acts of his appearing to be done in conſequence of this Power and Commiſſion; as for Inſtance. His Excluding *Simon Magus* from the Benefit of Chriſtianity, *Acts* 8. 20. *Thou haſt neither Part nor Lot in this Matter, for thy heart is not right before God.* Which Words are by Men of Learning, ſuppoſed ſpoken with

an

an Authority, Excluding him from all Part and Lot therein. And even in the very Inflance mentioned in the *Expofiti-on,* when he firft *opened* a *Door* to the *Gentiles* Preaching to *Cornelius*; there appears an Act of His, done in purfuance of this Commiffion, *viz.* the *Baptizing* him and his Houfhold, and judging them fit to be Baptized, notwithftanding they were *Gentiles,* therein admitting them, and alfo judging of their Right to be Admitted into the Church of Chrift, which was an Authoritative Act, and valid by his having the Power imply'd in the Charge of the Keys. But efpecially if it appear, as it will hereafter in this Difcourfe, that, as the Keys were given firft to St. *Peter,* and after to the Twelve Apoftles and to the Church, (at leaft the Power therein imply'd) So, not only St. *Peter,* but the reft of the Apoftles, yea the whole Church have acted thereupon, as having fuch Power; It fhall not be enough to fay, as the Bifhop does in his *Expofition* in a faint Expreffion, *That under the Figure of the Keys the Power* of *Difcipline* may *be underftood,* but that by, and with the Keys, this Power is conveyed to the Church, and is become part of its Miniftry. And this being faid, I do not apprehend that I fhall be put much to my fhifts for diftinctions to juftify the

C 3

Ex-

The Church of England's Wish.

Expounding the Words *Kingdom of Heaven* to mean the Church of Christ, and the *Keys* to be the Power of Discipline therein; having need of only one distinction to help me, if I should go further, and Expound the *Kingdom of Heaven* to mean our Eternal Happiness, and the Keys to imply a Power relating even to that, namely, That the Power then is not to be understood to be *Absolute*, as in our Saviour Christ, but *Ministerial*, as in Persons Acting under our Lord, with Limits upon their Power from the Conditions of his Gospel.

But again, As for that of *Binding* and *Loosing*, and the *Confirming in Heaven* what should be done in *Earth* by virtue of this Power. The *Exposition*, Page 190. Saith thus, " The Words *Binding* and " *Loosing* are used by the *Jewish* Writers, " in the Sense of Affirming or Denying " the Obligation of any Precept of the " *Law* that might be in Dispute; so according to this common form of Speech, " and the Sense formerly given of the " Words *Kingdom of Heaven*, the meaning of these Words must be, That Christ " Committed to his Apostles the Dispensing " his Gospel to the World, by which he Au- " thorized them to Dissolve the Obligation " of the *Mosaical Laws*, and to give other " Laws

"Laws to the *Christian* Church, which they
"should do under such visible Characters
"of a Divine Authority, Impowring and
"Conducting them in it, that it should be
"very Evident that what they did on Earth
"should be Ratify'd in Heaven. These
"Words thus understood carry in them a
"clear sense which agrees with the whole
"Design of the Gospel. But this Sense,
how clear soever, was too far fetch'd to be
Insisted on immediately as the only Sense
of the Words. Therefore the *Exposition*
says further very truly. "But *whatsoever*
"*may be their Sense*, there was nothing
"given particularly to St. *Peter* by them,
"which was not likewise given to the rest
"of the Apostles; Intimating, that they
might bear another Sense: Nevertheless,
Page 274. To prevent this Scripture from
being made use of as an Argument for
Confession of Sins to be made to a Priest
on account of a Power supposed in the Ministers of Christ's Church to bind and
loose Men's Sins, the *Exposition* saith, That
"the Power of *Binding* and *Loosing* given to
"the Apostles had been shewn on another
"Head, to belong to other matters, (therein
referring, as I suppose, to what had been
Argued of this Matter in *Page* 190.)
  I agree with the Reverend Bishop of *Sa-*
rum, you may be sure in this, that *what-*

soever

foever their Senfe may be, there was noth___
given particularly to St. *Peter* by them,
which was not likewife given to the reft of
the Apoftles, and likewife that there's no abfolute Neceffity for Confeffion of a Man's
Sins to be made to the Prieft in order to
their being Forgiven: inward Repentance
with Confeffion to God alone, fo it be fincere, and effectual to the Reforming of that
which a Man Repents of for the future,
doubtlefs qualifying for Pardon of Sin
with God, whether Confeffion be made
thereof to the Church or not, and without any Act of its Miniftry paffing upon
it. But by no means can I fubmit to acknowledge that his Lordfhip has given the
true or proper Senfe of the Words *Binding* and *Loofing.* For I have faid and fhewn
before, that the Words *Kingdom of Heaven*
mean fomewhat elfe than Preaching the
Gofpel, *viz.* Chrift's Church gathered
thereby: and fo have taken off one Argument upon which the *Expofition* groundeth
the new Senfe it hath given to thefe Words.
I fubmit to the Bifhop's Learning in this,
that the Terms of *Binding* and *Loofing* are
ufed by the *Jews,* to fignifie the Declaring
of what is Prohibited or Permitted by the
Law; but it fhall not hence follow that
Chrift hereby Committed to his Apoftles
the Difpenfing of his Gofpel to the World,
and

Authorized them to Diſſolve the Obligation of the *Moſaical* Laws, and to give other Laws to the *Chriſtian* Church under the Characters of a Divine Authority, Evidencing that what they did on Earth ſhould be Ratify'd in Heaven. For tho' this be a Truth, that Chriſtianity has voided the Obligation of the Law of *Moſes,* and that the Laws of Chriſt and the Apoſtles are now Laws to the Church, and Confirmed by a Divine Authority ; Nevertheleſs it ſhall be no eaſie thing to infer this Truth from this Power of *Binding* and *Looſing* given by Chriſt to his Apoſtles : This would be no Argument to a *Jew,* and is very little of an Argument to a *Chriſtian,* who can very hardly underſtand, I am perſwaded, our Lord intending in theſe his Words to overthrow the *Moſaick* Law ; and I know of none that ever alledged this Scripture for ſuch a Purpoſe. But indeed the Correſpondence between the Law and the Goſpel muſt be allowed to infer from the uſual ſignification of the Words *Binding* and *Looſing* among the *Jews,* what the Biſhop of *Sarum* would not willingly allow thoſe that Diſpute Controverſies for the Church of *Rome,* which yet they may Challenge, Namely, the Power of making Laws to be convey'd to the Church by this Power of *Binding* and *Looſing* given by our Lord to to his Apostles : That as there was a Power under the Law to determine Cases in dispute, and to decide what was Lawful and Unlawful, according to *Deut.* 17. 12. So the Power of *Binding* and *Loosing* here given the Church shall be understood of a like Power and Authority in the Church of Christ, to determine upon Cases that may arise, and oblige its Members to submit to her Judgment and Decisions. Yet this shall not serve however, the Purpose of the *Romanists*, because this Power and the Effect of it shall be limited to those things which after the Preaching of our Lord's Gospel remained for his Apostles and Disciples as well as their Assistants and Successors, to Determine and Appoint for the Framing of God's Church, and for the Conduct and Government of the same in Christianity; so that nothing of this Authority shall be advanc'd to the prejudice of that Gospel Truth, or the Religion of Jesus Christ, antecedent to this Authority it self; in dependance upon which, as well as in subservience thereto, this Authority is to Proceed and Act.

But neither do I take this to be the Primary or Proper Sense of the Words, (though I own it deducible from, and in some sort included therein) but that the *Power* of *Binding* and *Loosing* being expressed

preſſed to be Granted by, and with the *Keys* of God's Houſe; by *Binding* and *Looſing* ſhall be meant the *Opening* or *Shutting* the *Doors of his Church,* that is, the Admitting into, or Excluding out of it; So as *Binding* ſhall ſignify the Shutting out of the Church for Sin, and *Looſing*, the Admitting into the Church, or retaining in the Church as free from Sin. And as Admitting to, and Excluding from the Church is, or ought to be a Juſt and Lawful Preſumption of Admitting or Excluding from Heaven; in that reſpect its ſaid, that *Whatſoever is Bound on Earth ſhall be Bound in Heaven, and whatſoever is Looſed on Earth, ſhall be Looſed in Heaven,* intimating, that Men that are *Bound* or *Looſe,* as to the Church, are ſo really as to God : The ſame Thing or Things Morally and Legally Entitling to Heaven as to the Church, obtaining Remiſſion of Sins according to the Goſpel, and Entitling to the Sacraments of the Church, aſſuring that Remiſſion, making an Heir of Life Everlaſting and a Chriſtian; and on the other hand, deſerving to be Excluded Heaven if deſerving to be Excluded the Church, to be ſhut out from God's Pardon, if deſerving to be denied the hopes of it by the Church, and Excluding from his Heavenly Kingdom, if deſerving to be Excluded from the Church

of

of Chrift and Privileges of the fame. And that this is the fenfe of the Words *Binding* and *Loofing,* appears not only from what was fuppofed before by me, of the Church proceeding to *Bind* or *Loofe,* according as Men fhall *hear* or not *hear* what it fhall fay to them in reference to what may have been done by them contrary to their Chriftian Duty : But likewife from all that fhall be fhewn hereafter in this Difcourfe of the Practice of the Apoftles, and of the Church agreeably to this Senfe of the Words.

But again, as for that other Scripture which I have faid to be a Ground for Ecclefiaftical Difcipline, *Tell the Church* ; The Bifhop of *Sarum* in his Expofition of the 33*d.* Article (Referring to Excommunication, and Perfons Excommunicate, who are to be looked on as *Heathens,* &c.) Saith thus, " Though thefe Words of " our Saviour, of *telling the Church,* may " perhaps not be fo ftrictly applica- " ble to this Matter in their primary " Senfe as our Saviour firft fpoke them, " yet the Nature of Things, and the Pa- " rity of Reafon may well lead us to con- " clude, That though thefe Words did " immediately relate to the Compofing of " Private Differences, and of delating " intractable Perfons to the Synagogues, " yet they may be well extended to all " thofe

Expofit. 39th. Arr. P. 267.

The Church of England's Wish.

" thofe Publick Offences which are Inju-
" ries to the whole Body, and may be
" now apply'd to the *Chriftian Church*, and
" to the Paftors and Guides of it, though
" they related to the Synagogue when
" they were firft fpoken. I agree that the
Words as fpoken by our Lord, immediately
relate to the compofing of private Differences, for nothing can be plainer, (to ufe the
Bifhop of *Sarum*'s own Words in another
place) than that " Our Saviour was
" fpeaking of fuch private Differences as
" might arife among Men, and of the
" practice of forgiving Injuries, and com-
" pofing their Differences. *If thy Brother*
" *Sin againft thee; Firft*, Private Endea-
" vours were to be ufed; then the Inter-
" pofition of Friends was to be tried;
" and Finally, the Matter was to be re-
" ferred to the Body, or Affembly to which
" they belonged: And thofe who could
" not be gained by fuch Methods, were
" no more to be efteemed Brethren, but
" were to be looked on as very bad Men,
" like Heathens. But then I am not to grant
that our Saviour fends his Difciples to the
Synagogue, but to his own Church, and
affirm this to be the ground of that courfe
which appears to have been fetled in the
Church at *Corinth*, by the Blame St. *Paul*
charges them with for *going to Law before*
Infidels,

Infidels, 1 Cor. 6. 1; 2. For how should he blame them for that which they had not had some Order before not to do? What made them blame-worthy in this case, must be their having knowledge that their Differences ought to be ended within themselves, by those who were appointed to judge thereof within their own Body. It is indeed true that the *Jews,* in their Dissentions, had a Jurisdiction to this purpose in their Synagogues, and 'tis not unlikely that *putting out of the Synagogue* was the Punishment by which they enforced the Sentences of this kind; to the end that their Causes might not be carry'd always to the Courts of the Heathen, among whom they lived, as a scattered People, without Civil Power, lest God's Name should be Blasphemed from, and the *Gentiles* Scandalized at their Differences. Now be it always allowed, that for the same causes, our Lord (being willing also to follow the Example of the Synagogue) here estateth the same Power on his Church; it shall not thence follow, that our Lord sent his Disciples and Followers to the *Jewish Synagogue,* but to their own Church, *i. e* to the Assembly of *Christians,* to the Body or Assembly to which they belonged being now his Disciples. And that the Disciples should thus understand

stand our Lord, we have reason to think, he having said to *Peter* before, *upon this Rock will I Build my Church*, wherein he could not be understood of Building the *Synagogue*, which *Moses* had Built so long before, but must be understood, as purposing to Build a Church of his own; and consequently, to direct his Disciples to refer their Matters to this his Church. And the Order we find afterwards taken for a Report accordingly, is yet a more sure Evidence of his being thus understood. And this being said, it is indeed *Parity of Reason* that must lead us to conclude, That the Church of Christ having Power to call Men to account for these Matters, may much more call them to an account for such their deeds as shall be notorious Violations of the Christianity they have Professed; yet not Parity of Reason alone from this Scripture, but from this Scripture considered together with the Practice of the Church, calling these things to account at all times thereupon. And as the Bishop saith, that those who refused to hear the Church, *Page* 205. " might, upon such refractoriness be *Ex-* " *communicated*, and Prosecuted afterwards " in Temporal Courts, since they had by " their Perverseness forfeited all sort of " Right to that Tenderness and Charity " that

" that is due to true Chriſtians. I ſay the
ſame, but not in the ſenſe of ſome, who
have ſaid that Excommunication was no
other than an allowance to Sue ſuch a one
in the Heathen Courts : But that it was indeed in effect Lawful to Sue ſuch a one
in the Heathen Courts, as being no longer
a Chriſtian ; his Excommunication at the
ſame time having a much worſe Effect, as
to the ſtate of his Soul, in his being cut
off from the Church, and thereby from
the Right which Chriſtians have to God's
Promiſes. And I ſay alſo farther, That,
as in this place our Lord gave his Church
Power to *Excommunicate* thoſe who would
not ſtand to the Sentence of the Church
in their particular Differences ; much more
has the Church hereby power to Excommunicate thoſe who violate the Chriſtianity which they have Profeſſed, by Sins of
a deeper guilt, according to what hath
been practiſed by the Church in all Ages.
And thus the Inference that I build upon
parity of Reaſon, and the nature of Things,
I think not to be by much ſo Remote as
that the Biſhop leaves us to make from the
Power and Practice of the Synagogue, but
to ſtand upon much firmer ground, as ſuppoſing an Authority Eſtabliſhed by Chriſt
in the Church it ſelf, for the foundation of
what may appear done by the Church in
virtue of that Authority. Again

Again, as for the Words of our Saviour, *Whofoever Sins ye remit, they are remitted* Jo. 20. 23. *unto them, and whofoever Sins ye retain, they are retained*; it fo happens that I muft have fome Conteft with the *Bifhop of Sarum* about their Senfe alfo. The *Expofition* debating about the matter of Expofit. *Penance*, recites an Opinion holding 39 Art. (rightly and for my Purpofe) that the Power P.g. 274 given the Apoftles, when our Saviour *brea-* 275, 276. *thed* on them and gave them the *Holy Ghoft*, and with that told them, that *Whof·ever Sins they remitted, they were remitted, and whofoever Sins they retained, they were re-tained*; was not a Perfonal Thing, or an Extraordinary and Miraculous Authority given to the Apoftles, and to them only, with the effufion of the Holy Ghoft; but a Minifterial Authority ftill to be con-tinued in the Church, which the Succeffors of the Apoftles, the Minifters of Chrift's Church, by the affiftance of the Holy Ghoft ever abiding with, and in the Church may execute and effect. More-over, the *Expofition* argueth againft an Er-roneous Opinion (pretending hence that the Church hath an abfolute and unlimit-ed Power in this matter) no lefs rightly than ftrongly, that all the Conditions ex-preffed in the Gofpel as qualifying for Par-don of Sin, are Limits upon this Power,

D obliging

obliging the Ministers of Christ's Church not to pretend of themselves to an absolute Power of retaining and remitting Sins; but to act with an Eye having regard to those Conditions in all they shall do of this nature. But when after this the *Exposition* comes to say, " Thus we think " we are fully justified by saying, That by " these words our Saviour did indeed fully " impower his Apostles to publish his " Gospel to the World, and to declare the " Terms of Salvation, and of obtaining " the Pardon of Sin, in which they were " to be Infallibly assisted, so that they " could not err in discharging their Com- " mission; and the Terms of the Cove- " nant of Grace being thus settled by " them, all who were to succeed them, " were also impowered to go on with the " Publication of this Pardon; so that " whatsoever they declared in the Name " of God, conform to the Tenor of that " which the Apostles were to settle, " should be always made good. We do " also acknowledge that the Pastors of " the Church have in the way of Censure " and Government, a Ministerial Autho- " rity to remit or to retain Sins, as they are " *matters of scandal or offence : though that* " *indeed does not seem to be the meaning of* " *those words of our Saviour.; and* there- " fore

" fore we think that the Power of Par-
" doning is only Declaratory; so that all
" the Exercises of it are then only Effectual,
" when the Declarations of the Pardon
" are made conform to the conditions of
" the Gospel.   I cannot by any means, be
of Opinion, that the *Bishop* of *Sarum* ought
to have said or intimated as concerning
the Sense of the *Church of England* about
this matter ; That this supposeth, that by
these words, *Whosoever Sins ye remit*, &c.
our Saviour only did impower his Apostles
to publish his Gospel, and to declare the
Terms of Pardon and Salvation ; and the
Terms being by them settled, did herein
impower their Successors to go on with
the Publication of this Pardon, and whatsoever they declared in the Name of God
conform to the Tenor of the Terms thus
settled should be made good.   For though
this be indeed all true; and probably also
implied in those words of our Saviour :
Yet it is not to be thought that a Church
claiming the Power of Excommunication,
and a Right of remitting and retaining
Sins Authoritatively, should understand
our Saviour not to mean or intend the
giving an Authority for such Purpose in
these words.   On the contrary, in proof
that the *Church of England* understandeth
those words of our Saviour to be the foun-

dation of a Ministerial Authority, for the remitting and retaining Sins, I offer her own words in the *Ordination of Priests.* " Receive the Holy Ghost for the Office " and Work of a Priest in the Church of " God, *&c. Whose Sins thou dost forgive,* " *they are forgiven, and whose Sins thou* " *dost retain, they are retained.* And be " thou a faithful Dispenser of the Word of " God and of his Holy Sacraments; in " the Name of the Father, and of the " Son, and of the Holy Ghost. Wherein from its having applied these words of our Saviour, as giving Authority, and Commissioning for the Office and Work of a Priest; and immediately subjoining a charge concerning the particulars of this Office to him that had this committed to him; *To be a faithful* Dispenser of the *word of God,* and of his *Holy Sacraments*; it appeareth, that as the Church of *England* understood these words of our Lord, to have given Authority for the dispensing *of his word, and preaching of his Gospel*; so it understands them also as authorizing the Dispensation of the *Holy Sacraments:* The faithful dispensing of which shall ever be understood to imply; the witholding of the Sacraments, and therein witholding the hopes of God's Mercy and Pardon from Persons guilty of known Sins; inconsistent confiftent with Chriftianity; as well as the Miniftration of the fame, in affurance of God's Favour and Pardon of Sin, to thofe that live according to their Holy Profeffion. And the Difpenfation of Difcipline, for the remitting and retaining Sin being thus implied in the difpenfing of the Sacraments, and the one fuppofed authorized by this Commiffion of our Saviour's as well as the other; we may well fuppofe to be the Reafon of one of the Queftions, demanded of him that defires the Office of a Prieft; *viz.* " Will you " give your faithful diligence always, fo " to Minifter the *Doctrine* and *Sacraments,* " and the *Difcipline of Chrift* as the Lord " hath commanded? And whereas the *Bifhop of Sarum* fpeaking feemingly on the behalf, and in the name of the Church of *England,* faith, " We acknowledge that " the Paftors of the Church have in the " way of Cenfure or Government, a Mi- " nifterial Authority to remit, or to re- " tain Sins, as they are matters of fcan- " dal or offence; though that indeed does " not feem to be the meaning of thefe " words of our Saviour. I do not think it ought to have been faid, that (holding the Opinion the Church of *England* holds about the matter) we acknowledge that Paftors have in the way of Cenfure and

Government a Ministerial Authority to remit or to retain Sins ; meaning this only as they are matters of *scandal* and *offence* : much less in the Sense intimated by the Bishop, *Pag.* 274. where he says, " We " (meaning the Church) as a Body that " may be offended with the Sins of others, " forgive the Scandals committed against " the Church. And again, " We as the " Officers of the Church, authorized for " that End, do forgive all the Offences " and Scandals committed by them against " the whole Body. This would intimate the Authority of the Church to have an hand in the remitting and retaining Sins, no otherwise than as it may forgive the Offence and Scandal as to its self, not the Sin as to God. I think the Bishop may say truly of this, *that it seemeth not to be the meaning of our Saviour's words, Whosoever Sins ye remit,* &c. to give foundation to such an Authority. For what the breathing on his Apostles, and giving them the Holy Ghost, to give them thereby an Authority for such a purpose should mean, will be hard to shew. But taking the Authority of the Church as it is, and hath been always thought to be, a Power of remitting or retaining Sins ; taking away the guilt of them as to God, or leaving them to his Punishment ; there shall be

need

need of the *Holy Ghost*, as well to evidence this Authority to be from God, as to direct them that have the Miniftry of this Authority to do it aright, and to bring it to effect. And there fhall be reafon to think that thefe words of our Saviour are a warrant to that Authority in his Church, which acteth under God to this purpofe, and were by him defigned to be fo: Efpecially feeing that this Act of his Church doth really more to the immediate purpofe of remitting and retaining Sins, than any other Act of its Miniftry: For the Preaching of the Gofpel, indeed acquainteth Men upon what Conditions God's Pardon is to be had; but this engageth them in the courfe that obtaineth it. But to look fomewhat more into the Bifhop's Notion of the Church's remitting Sins, as matter of fcandal and offence, fuppofing it to call Offenders to account, for fatisfaction to its felf, in refpect of the offence, and remitting Sin, as forgiving the offence as to it felf, not the Sin as to God: The Notion is new and fingular, and I can fee little or no ground to think that the Church ever pretended her Miniftry to this purpofe, or authorized Perfons to forgive after fuch a manner, in the name of the Body. That the Church as a Body is concerned to forgive Scandals,

after

after the manner that particular Persons are to forgive their Brethrens Trespasses ; or that for Peace and Quiet of Conscience sake, a Sinner is obliged to seek Pardon from the Church, as a Body offended, as a Man is to seek Reconciliation with his injured Brother, I am yet to learn. And if it should be thus, it would afford a much better Argument for the necessity of confessing Sins to the Church, than any that I have known made use of by those that dispute for it on behalf of the *Church of Rome.* It is indeed true, that the Church receiveth offence from all visible Sins. But how differeth that from what every Man receiveth, when he seeth his Brother Sin against God ? What meaneth then the Church's formal Pardon in such case ? Indeed as the Church is a Body, and hath in charge the Government of its Members in Christianity, it is concerned to remove scandals from the Body, by removing scandalous Persons from the Society ; and may require to be satisfied of a more Christian behaviour in offenders for the future, or otherwise not allow them to continue in the Society. But to require satisfaction from offenders, as a Man requireth satisfaction for injuries done him, was never the Reason of Penance in the Church of Christ ; nor doth the Church pretend to

remit

remit Sins, by giving its own Pardon, but by affuring God's. Accordingly the Abfolution the Church of *England* giveth to dying Penitents, tendeth to affure the Mercy of God, for the forgivenefs of their offences againft him ; but pretendeth not this Mercy to follow from any forgivenefs, which the Church as a Body offended can or doth give them ; but as her Prayers may prevail with Chrift, who hath left Power to his Church to Abfolve all Sinners who truly Repent ; and as having a Minifterial Power trufted with it by God, to affure his Mercy to fuch as it can prefume to be truly Penitent ; it thereupon affureth it to them, upon the ground it hath to prefume of their Repentance. The Senfe of our Church alfo, as concerning the End of Difcipline, appeareth in the Preface to the *Commination*, where it faith it was anciently ufed ; *That the Souls of fuch* as were put to Penance *might be faved in the day of the Lord, and that others admonifhed by their Example might be afraid to offend.* In fhort, 'tis undeniable that the Authority given the Church for *Government*, was in the defign of Chrift, a *means of Salvation*, as much as any other part of the Miniftry committed to it, and confequently what the Church ought to feek by its Difcipline, is the *faving of Souls*

from

See the Abfolution in Vifitation of the Sick.

from Death : And if the scandal of bad example be thereby taken away from the Body of Christians, as it will be by the Removal of scandalous Persons from the Society ; or by procuring their amendment (for then the scandal that may be cast upon it from without is prevented, and the offence within ceaseth) this is accidental, and not to be accounted as the End of the Church's Ministry, being the least considerable part of the aim in it. Whosoever will look into the way and method of the Antient Church, in putting Sinners under Penance, and releasing them from it ; or into the mention which Ecclesiastical Writers make of the practice of Penance, and nature of it, shall be sure to find the Church in this work of her Ministry, not to have gone about to oblige offenders to ask Pardon of the Body, nor to have offered them Pardon as of and from it self ; but to have laboured always by Exhortations, by Reproofs, and by Censures to bring offenders to the sight and acknowledgment of their Faults ; constraining them to a due course of Humiliation, for procuring forgiveness of God : Shall find also the Penitents submitting to go through the course of Humiliation, enjoined them in hope of God's forgiveness ; and soliciting the Church to interceed

interceed with God on their behalf, and the Prayers of the Church allowed and granted them for that purpose, during the Time of their Penance: Shall find likewise the Penitential Acts enjoined, to be such Acts of Humiliation, Mortification, and self-denial, as could be thought most effectual to humble the Sinner in respect of his Sins; to work in him a Godly sorrow, and to work him off from the Love of Sin, or most likely to prevail with God for Mercy; on which account works of Charity were sometimes prescribed, in hope that by means of such works, ever acceptable with God, they might sooner obtain Mercy. It shall be found also that the course of Penance prescribed was for a longer or shorter Time, as Mens Crimes and Guilt were thought to be greater or less; from which the Church reasonably concluded a greater or less difficulty to obtain Reconciliation with God, and the Recovery of his Favour: And likewise that when the Church was satisfied of the Sinner's Repentance, it admitted him to the Sacraments and Privileges of God's Church; and therein assured his hopes as touching God's Mercy and Pardon. In all which it appears that the Great concern of the Church, is for the Sinner's Soul, in this its Ministry, and

that

that herein the Church may be truly said to act according to, and to fulfil the Effect of our Saviour's Commission, in *remitting Sins*, as it Ministreth the means of forgiveness; and not only teacheth the course Men are to hold in seeking Pardon, but prescribeth it, and engageth them in it, and so helpeth them forward in the course that they obtain it. But nevertheless after all, this is not forgiving Sins as God forgiveth them, nor doth it suppose it to be in the Church to Pardon Sin, without that disposition, which in the Gospel qualifieth a Man for it; so that indeed, the Exercise of this Ministry in the Church (as the Bishop saith rightly) is then only effectual, when it is made *Conform to the Conditions of the Gospel:* and yet the Power of the Church in *remitting Sin* shall be more than *Declaratory,* as being *Ministerial,* having and acting with authority, in procuring Pardon by the means of Repentance, and in assuring the same.

And now I think my self to have fully vindicated the Scriptures hitherto cited, to their proper Sense, and so to be not only a good Foundation for an Authority in the Church, for the Ministring of Discipline, but an obligation also upon it to discharge this part of its Ministry.

Though

The Church of England's Wish.

Though it has not been without concern, that I have held this debate with so Reverend a Prelate of our own Church, especially, because I may not hold him as an Enemy, but a Friend in the cause of Church-Discipline, which he hath argued much for in divers places of that his Book: Which nevertheless bearing the Title of an *Expofition* of the 39 Articles of the Church of *England*, should in that respect be thought to have delivered the Sense of our Church, concerning those Scriptures, when they fell under consideration in any of the Articles that relate to the Government, Authority or Discipline of the Church. And if there were Reason to think the Church understood them in the Sense of the Bishop; I must not hope my Arguments should prevail with those that have share in the Ministry of the Church, to acknowledge themselves under any such obligation, to restore a Discipline therein, as I pretend them to be. This therefore, and my present undertaking, obliging me to seek beyond the usefulness and advantage of Discipline, a foundation for it in Scripture, (seeing that the Expediency thereof, or its Congruity to the Design of the Christian Religion, may not be looked on as sufficient of it self, to oblige the Church otherwise to restore it). have been
the

the fole Motives prevailing with me to undertake to retrieve thefe Scriptures to the Senfe, which in the Church of Chrift they have generally been underftood in, and which the Practice of the Apoftles, and of the whole Church inferreth.

C H A P. III.

HAving thus far fhewed the Foundation of Ecclefiaftical Power, and therein confequently of Difcipline the chief Act thereof, to have been laid by our Lord Chrift himfelf; 'twill be now requifite that we look into the Acts of the Apoftles and Difciples of our Lord thereupon; and likewife what Scriptures we have to fhew the Courfe and Order taken and fettled by them, for the Government of the Church, and for Difcipline therein.

Now though our Lord Chrift himfelf, as hath been fhewn, gave this Power and Authority to his Church for Government and Difcipline therein; yet we muft not expect to find the Exercife of it, whilft himfelf was upon Earth, his Church not being as yet Gathered. And for the fame Reafon the Acts of this Power, it is to be be suppofed were few, if any, for some time after the Apoftles began their Preaching of the Gofpel upon our Saviour's Afcenfion; for though they might underftand our Lord to have given a power to his Church, and knew themfelves entrufted with the difcharge of it, yet they muft alfo *know* their Commiffion could not take place until a Church in his Name were Gather'd and Form'd. The Apoftles alfo and Difciples continued *in* the Synagogue with the *Jews* for a time, while there was hope of gaining thefe over to Chriftianity; in which fpace, though they had feparate Meetings, for which they were to do as Chriftians, yet the Body of the Church not being as yet Formed, there could not much appear of the Method and Way of Government therein. There is alfo a Reafon to be given why we have not many Inftances in the Scriptures of the New Teftament, of Offenders brought under Difcipline in the Church, or Cenfures upon the Refractory that would not: which is this, That the *Chriftian* Religion was then New, and the Churches not well Setled, and withal, thofe that then became *Chriftians* could not well come to the Church, but with a Refolution to undergo the Crofs, and fuffer Perfecution, (the Church then being Perfecuted on every fide, hated alike by *Jew* and *Gentile*) and such a Resolution, 'tis likely, would not soon depart from the *Christianity* it had undertaken to live after, as well as constantly to profess; and so the Offenders 'tis very probable were not many. Moreover, the Apostles had not only Power and Authority to Censure Transgressors, but an extraordinary power to punish Hypocrites, and such as were so wicked as to Despise God and his Church, and Disobey the Gospel of his Son, with Plagues, Diseases, and Death, as in the Case of *Ananias* and *Saphira*, so that in their time few Hypocrites durst offer themselves to become *Christians*; and the Professors of *Christianity*, it must be supposed had greater regard to live as their Holy Profession obliged them, in respect of the imminent danger, should they transgress, and not walk after the holy Commandment delivered unto them. According to what is said, *Acts* 5. 11. upon what befell *Ananias* and *Saphira*, that *great fear came upon all the Church, and upon as many as heard these things.* Moreover, neither may we expect in the Instances that are of this nature in the New Testament, an Account at large of the Course and Order taken by the Apostles, concerning Government and Discipline in the Churches of their Planting,

ing, but only References therein to some Course and Order taken. For neither do we find the whole of the Christian Doctrine delivered together in any of these Scriptures, they being occasional Epistles sent to Churches that were before Instructed in Christianity, and had a Summary or Form of Doctrine delivered to them before, of which mention is often made, and frequent reference thereto had therein. And so the Order taken, and Course setled in the Churches about Government and Discipline, is not to be supposed expressed, but referred to as occasion was, from the matter and subject about which the Apostles had occasion to Write to the Churches. But nevertheless these References are as much an Evidence of an Order setled to this purpose, as if we had that Order it self before our Eyes. Because it could not be, that the Apostles could write to their Churches, and refer to such Order or Course if such had not been, or had not been also such as their Writings intimate them. So that what we may gather to have been part of such Orders from Intimations in the Apostles Writings referring thereto, we have consequently the same reason to believe, as if we had the Order extant in their Writings, and therein saw it to be part. For believing the Apo-

E   stles ftles Men of common Senfe, and of fome Integrity, it is not to be thought they fhoul: write of things that were not, as though they were ; and efpecially fuppofing them affifted in their Writings by the Holy Ghoft, it can no more be thought that they fhould give falfe Suggeftions, or make falfe and wrong References, than that they fhould give us falfe relations, or unfaithful accounts of things.

But to the Scriptures that are for our Purpofe. I have occafionally faid before, that what St. *Peter* did in excluding *Simon Magus*, difcovered a Counterfeit Chriftian from the benefit of Chriftianity, feems to be an Act of the Power of the Keys committed to him. For when he faith, *Acts* 8. 21. *Thou haft neither Part nor Lot in this Matter,* &c. it feems to be fpoken with an Authority excluding him from all that *part* and *lot* that he might have had together with other Believers by his being Baptized, had he not given S. *Peter* caufe to Judge of him, from the difcovery of the thought of his wicked heart, That *he was in the gall of bitternefs* and *in the bond of iniquity;* and when immediately upon this Rebuke and Cenfure, he bids him *Repent of this his Wickednefs, and pray God if perhaps the thought of his heart might be forgiven,* It may be underftood indeed that he left him

to

to his liberty for this; but I should rather think that he left him to expect God's Judgment if he did it not: And the answer of *Simon, Pray ye to the Lord for me, that none of these things which ye have spoke come upon me.*; seems as though his fear of the consequences of S. *Peter*'s Censure had driven him to seek to that Authority which had Pronounced so of him to intercede with God on his behalf, that the Evil might not come upon him. This therefore is very like to, if not the same with what was usually done in the Church, as to the Censure of Offenders, and putting them under a necessity of Repentance, if they would escape God's Judgments, who were thereupon driven by their fear, to seek God's Pardon, and to desire the Prayers of his Church to be Offered to God on their behalf, in commiseration and pity of their circumstances, as they lay under great guilt, and thereby were fallen under the dreadful expectation of the Wrath and Judgment of God. But let every one think of this as he pleaseth; it shall not be deny'd me, that as what St. *Paul* did in *delivering to Satan* the Incestuous Person at *Corinth* was an Act of this Power *of the Keys*; so what he there argueth with that Church concerning the 1 Cor. Removal of *that Person from among them,*

E 2 sup-

ſuppoſeth and referreth to ſome Order
known before unto, or ſetled before in
that Church for the *putting away from am ng
them ſuch wicked Perſons.* For what elſe
meaneth that which he ſaith, *I verily as*
abſent in Body, but preſent in Spirit, have
judged already as though I were preſent; con-
cerning him that hath ſo done this deed; In
the Name of our Lord Jeſus *Chriſt, when ye*
are gathered together, and my Spirit with
the Power of our Lord Jeſus *Chriſt, to deli-*
ver ſuch a one unto Satan for the deſtruction
of the Fleſh, that the Spirit may be ſaved in
the Day of the Lord Jeſus ; but this, that
he being no leſs careful for them and the
concerns of their Church when abſent,
than when preſent, *that his care for them*
in the ſight of God might appear, wrote to
them about this matter, and *judged con-*
cerning him that had done this wicked
deed, *in the name of our Lord* Jeſus Chriſt,
that 'twas meet *when they* were *gathered*
together, to conſult and conſider the
thought and judgment of his Spirit thereupon, the Offender ſhould by them, and
the *Power which they had from our Lord* Jeſus Chriſt *for this purpoſe, be delivered un-*
to Satan for the deſtruction of the Fleſh, that
the Spirit might be ſaved in the Day of the
Lord, i. e. be Excommunicated and Removed from God's Church ? For 'tis evident

Verſe 3. 4

2 Cor. 7 12

dent that Excommunication was the thing
which the Apostle signified by *delivering
unto Satan.* For how could he mean other
than what he finds fault had not been done,
the taking away from among them him that Verse
had done that deed, and what he pref-
fes them by his Arguments to do, (not
knowing as yet what Obedience they
would yield to him in this matter); *to* Verse
purge out the old Leaven, and to *put away
from among themselves that wicked Person.* Verse
He might indeed defign to intimate, and
does very probably exprefs an extraordinary Effect that followed it in the
Apoftles time, to wit, That thofe which
were put out of the Church became v fibly fubject to Satan, inflicting Plagues
and Difeafes on their Bodies which
might reduce them to Repentance, which
the Apoftle calleth *the Deftruction of the
Flefh, that the Spirit may be Saved in the Day
of the Lord.* And there is reafon to think,
that the Apoftles had Power thus to Punifh
the Refractory, provided and given by
God, as the reft of his Miraculous Graces
to evidence his Prefence and Power in the
Church. Neverthelefs the *delivering to Satan* fhall firft mean, *the putting out of the
Church,* before it fignify the confequence
thereof, and this efpecially becaufe it fhall
be always a confequence, that whofoever

is *put out of God's Church,* shall fall under
the *Power of Satan* as to his Soul, when
it may be otherwise as to his Body; that
is, suppofing his being put out of the
Church work no effect on him towards
Repentance. And whereas we fee the
Judgment that S. *Paul* paffed in the cafe
was an act of Authority, being *in the
name of our Lord Jefus Chrift,* and that,
when he requireth them to Execute his
Sentence, he maketh mention of their
having alfo *Power from our Lord Jefus
Chrift* for that purpofe; Let it be fhewn
what other Power the Apoftle could have
from our Lord Jefus Chrift for this purpofe, or what other at leaft the Church
of *Corinth* could have for fuch purpofe;
or let the *Power of the Keys* given by Chrift
to his Church, be allowed to be the Power
by which this Act was done by S. *Paul,*
and enjoined by him upon the Church of
Corinth to be fully executed. And again,
when he layeth blame on the *Corinthians,*
that they *had not mourned to put away him
that had done this Evil deed from among
them;* as no other ground of blame could
lye againft them in this refpect, but fome
antecedent Order left with them to put
away fuch Offenders from among them,
which rendered them blameable, for that
they had not done according to it: So
what

what is said of their *not mourning: to put away*, being easily understood if we call to mind the Solemnity of Excommunication in the Primitive Church (which was to put the Person out of the Church with mourning) but not intelligible otherwise; this Circumstance or Ceremony shall hereupon cause the *putting away* to be expounded, to signifie *Excommunication*, as this Scripture shall again be a good Proof, that the Practice of Excommunication, as well as the Ceremony, had place in the Primitive Church, as being derived from the Apostles, who shall be acknowledged to have taken Order for the *Power of the Keys* to be executed in the Church, from the plain Reference which this Scripture hath to some such Order, and from the express mention therein of this Circumstance being part of it.

But we have more to our Purpose yet in this Chapter, when S. *Paul* tells the *Corinthians* that *he had wrote to them in an* Ve *Epistle not to company with Fornicators,* and explains himself, That he meant not they should forbear the Company of *Gentiles* for such Sins, of whom better could not be expected; but if a Christian lived in any of these Heathen Vices, they should not *keep company with such a one, no not to eat;* much more should they be concerned

to

to remove such from the Church (for this if I mistake not, is the form and force of his Argument;) for neither himself nor they had *to do to judge them that are without,* therefore such they must leave to God to judge; but they *might judge,* they had Power of judging *those that are within,* and this obliged them *to put away from among them that wicked Person.* Here the case is plain, there is Power in the Church to judge and take away offenders; and this Power being committed to the Church, is argued by the Apostle to be an obligation upon the Church, to put away him that had done Evil.

I shall not go off from the Scripture in hand, until I have considered what the Bishop of *Sarum* has said concerning it, in his Exposition of the 33. *Article* of the Church of *England,* relating to Persons *Excommunicate, viz.* " That the *Delivery* " *unto Satan* was visibly an Act of Mi- " raculous Power lodged with the Apostles. " That the Apostles never reckon this a- " mong the standing Functions of the " Church, nor do they give any charge " or directions about it; They used it " themselves, and but seldom. That " S. *Paul,* it's true, being carried by a " just Zeal against the scandal which the " Incestuous Person at *Corinth* had cast " upon

" upon the Christian Religion, did ad-
" judge him to this severe degree of Cen-
" sure. But he *judged it,* and did only
" order the *Corinthians* to publish it, as
" coming from him *with the Power of our*
" *Lord Jesus Christ*; that so the Thing
" might become the more Publick, and
" that the Effects of it might be more
" Conspicuous. That the Primitive Church,
" which being nearest the Fountain, did
" best understand the nature of Church
" Power and the Effects of her Censures,
" thought of nothing in this Matter; but
" of denying to suffer Apostates, or ra-
" ther scandalous Persons to mix with the
" rest in the Sacraments, or in the other
" parts of Worship, *&c.* Which agrees
" well with the Nature, and the Ends of
" Church-Power, which was given for
" *Edification,* and not for *Destruction,* &c.
" Whereas the other looks like a Power
" that designs *Destruction,* rather than *Edi-*
" *fication,* &c. I am not to say, that the
Bishop had not cause to find fault with
some that are over hasty to denounce *Ana-*
themaes, against all that differ in Opinion
from them in Doctrinal Points; but that
to shew or restrain the Abuse of Church-
Power in such Proceedings, he ought not
to have used such an Argument as this,
which weakens the Foundation of the due
Power

Power of the Church. I muſt therefore of neceſſity diſſent from the Biſhop in this that he ſuggeſts, *viz.* That the *Delivery unto Satan* was viſibly an Act of *Miraculous Power* lodged in the Apoſtles, ſuch an Act of *Apoſtolical Authority*, as is not to be made a *Precedent* for the ſtanding Practice of the Church. For if the Biſhop be in the right in this ſuggeſtion, I muſt be in the wrong, who have given this for an Inſtance of the *Power of the Keys* left by Chriſt with his Church, and for a Precedent to the Church to act upon that Power. What then are his Arguments? " The " Apoſtles (he ſaith) as they ſtruck ſome " *blind* or *dead*, ſo had an Authority of " letting looſe Evil Spirits on ſome, to " haunt and terrifie, or to puniſh and " plague them, *&c.* but they never reck- " on this among the ſtanding Functions " of the Church, nor give any charge or " directions about it: They uſed it them- " ſelves, and but ſeldom. To which I anſwer, If it be here meant, that the Apoſtles had Power and Authority to *let looſe Evil Spirits* upon Sinners, to plague and puniſh them, and that they did it, otherwiſe than as this was the Conſequence of their Cenſures, which removed ſuch out of the Church; it is a Suppoſition without *Proof*, of which I may ſay indeed with
the

the *Exposition*, that the Apostles never reckoned this among the *standing Functions* of the Church, nor gave charge or directions about it ; but cannot say as the *Exposition* does, *That they used it, and but seldom* ; being yet to learn that the Apostles ever made use of such a Power. Which nevertheless should it be proved to have been, will be nothing to the purpose : For S. *Paul's* Act in *delivering to Satan,* was most certainly a *Spiritual Censure* passed by himself, because the Church of *Corinth* had neglected to do their Duty in the case, for which neglect he highly blames them, and judges the offender himself, because they did not judged him : And though the blame he lays on them be for not *taking away* from among them him that had done the Evil deed, and himself judgeth that he be *delivered to Satan* ; yet is there Reason to think that he meaneth the same thing, and did no other than what he blameth them for not having done : For having charged it upon them to execute his Censure, not as yet knowing what Obedience they would yeild to him therein, he presseth them by several Arguments to it, and at last concludes with this ; *Therefore put away from among your selves that wicked Person :* i. e. That they should now therefore do that in executing his Sentence,

tence, which they ought to have done of themselves before. But now if it be meant in the *Exposition*, That the *Putting out of the Church*, which was a Spiritual Cenfure, had alfo another Effect in the time of the Apoftles, as there did fome Vifible or Corporal vexation of fuch Perfons by Evil Spirits enfue ; this is a Conjecture that feemeth to have fome ground, and therefore as I have allowed it before, fo I here own it for an Effect of *Miraculous Power* granted among others, by God for the firft confirmation of the Gofpel, and for evidence of his Prefence and Power in the Church, as well as for enforcing the Miniftry of the Church to its intended Purpofes. I therefore likewife acknowledge, that the Apoftles do not affure this Effect to the Spiritual Cenfures of the Church in all times, neither have they given Directions to the Church to pretend to a Power for fuch Purpofe, or to ufe its Authority in any cafe, in expectation of any fuch Event. But then I cannot fay, That the Apoftles *ufed this* and *but feldom*; forafmuch, as it appears not to me, that they put out of the Church fometimes with purpofe that this Effect fhould follow, and fometimes not ; but only that this Effect followed in as many cafes as it pleafed God, to fhew his giving effect to

the

the Miniftry of his Church, by inflicting this Extraordinary Punifhment. And this Effect having followed as often and as long as God thought fit, to prevent Mens having his Inftitutions in Contempt; it ceafed afterwards when the Divine Wifdom thought enough done to convince the World, that God would give Power and Efficacy to the Miniftry of his Church, fufficient to accomplifh the Ends whereunto it was defigned. Be it allowed therefore, that this Extraordinary Effect following the Spiritual Cenfures of the Apoftles was from a *Miraculous Power* ; it fhall not any wife follow, hereupon, that S. Paul's Act in *delivering to Satan* the Inceftuous Perfon at *Corinth*, was an Act of *Miraculous Power*, not to be made a Prefident for the Practice of the Church : For as it was a Cenfure that *put* the Offender *out of the Church*, it fhall be a Prefident for the Church of God always to follow ; and though the Church may not have fufficient ground, thence to expect that every Perfon thus *put out* fhall be plagued by fome *Evil Spirit*, yet fhall this very Effect following upon the Apoftle's Act, confirm the Faith of the Church in the Execution of its Miniftry ; That the Sentence of the Church paffed *in the name of our Lord Jefus Chrift*, and executed as

by

by his Power, so according to his **Will**, shall have its Effect ; because it is *His*, who having shewn his Power by visible Effects, shall be thought able to work his Purposes in a way not visible. Besides, it shall not be denied me, that the Censure that *putteth out of the Church* is properly a *Delivering to Satan*, if visible Vexation of such Persons by Evil Spirits never did ensue, in respect of other and worse Effects, which may justly, and are always to be expected and feared, by such as are duly and regularly cast out of the Church of God by that Censure, *viz.* Satan's having Power over their Souls, to lead them Captive to Sin at his Will, and to hold them as a sure Possession to himself : Which yeilds but too great a Reason, why he may be said to be *delivered to Satan*, who is put out of the Church. What is said in the *Exposition*, therefore hath proved nothing hitherto to the contrary, but that S. *Paul's* Act may be a President for the Church to act upon the *Power of the Keys*, and to *put away* and *deliver to Satan by putting away* Scandalous and Refractory Sinners. And what it saith of the Apostles not reckoning this among the *standing functions* of the Church, nor giving directions about it, is confuted by this very Act of the Apostle, and the Circumstances

cumſtances thereof; for as much as there
muſt have been ſome antecedent Order,
or Inſtructions to the Church of *Corinth,*
for the thus cenſuring Offenders; otherwiſe, Why are they blamed? and after
S. *Paul* had paſſed the Sentence himſelf,
becauſe they had not done it as they ought,
we ſee he giveth charge about it, in charging them to execute it; and in perſiſting
ſtill to require of them, that they *put a-
way* from among them that *wicked Perſon,*
1 Cor. 5. 13. But the *Expoſition* ſaith of
S. *Paul's* adjudging the Offender to this
ſevere degree of Cenſure. " That he *judg-
" ed it,* and did only order the *Corinthians*
" to *publiſh* it, as coming from him *with*
" *Power from our Lord Jeſus Chriſt:* That
" ſo the Thing might become the more
" Publick, and that the Effects of it might
" be the more Conſpicuous. Intimating
that the Sentence was an *Apoſtolical Act,*
ſuch as the *Corinthians* had not Power to
judge themſelves, and which alſo they were
the Apoſtles Inſtruments to *publiſh only,*
as coming from him with the Power of
our Lord Jeſus Chriſt; and that S. *Paul*
made uſe of them therein, not for any
thing they had to do in the matter, but
only that the Thing might thereby be
made more Publick, and the Effects more
Conſpicuous. Which is all miſtake: For
if

if the Church of *Corinth* had not *Power from our Lord Jefus Chrift* to *put away* him that had done this Deed, Why are they blamed ? And what S. *Paul* did in *judging* concerning him that had done this Deed, he faith was *in the name of our Lord Jefus Chrift,* therein intimating his own Act to be by Power from him ; when afterwards he requires of them to execute it, *when they were gathered together.* and his *Spirit, with the Power of our Lord Jefus Chrift,* he feems rather to tell them that they had Power from Chrift of themfelves, to put the Sentence in Execution, than that he now gave them a Power for it ; as appears moft plainly, when he faith afterwards, *Do not ye judge them that are within ?* Therein demanding whether they did not understand their Power, and requiring them immediately to act upon it, and *put away from among them that wicked Perfon.* And to fay , Therefore that S. *Paul* made ufe of them in this cafe, *only that the Thing might be the more Publick, and the Effects more Confpicuous,* is fpeaking without Book ; there appearing nothing from the Text of fuch purpofe in S. *Paul,* no Confpicuous Effects of this Act in any vifible Punifhment of the Offender remembred , to give ground for this conjecture. I may certainly upon much better grounds offer a conjecture,

Cor. 5.4.

V. 12.

V. 13.

conjecture, That the Apostle made use of them to execute this his Sentence, that their having an hand therein might take away the Sin and Scandal, that lay upon the Church of *Corinth*, or those that were concerned by their Office at least to act for that Church, for not having done it before: or because the Sentence being the *putting away* the Offender out of the Church, it could not take place without them, who were the Assembly from which he was to be removed (upon which ground the People always had an Interest and concern in such Censures in the Primitive Times, these and indeed all Publick Acts of the Church passing at the Publick Assemblies of the same). But the *Exposition* saith further; " The Primitive " Church, that being nearest the Fountain, " did best understand the Nature of " Church Power, and the Effects of the " same, thought of nothing in this mat- " ter, but of denying Apostates, or ra- " ther Scandalous Persons to mix with " the rest in the Sacrament, or in the " other parts of Worship. If this be in- tended to suggest, that the Primitive Church thought that which S. *Paul* did in this case, to be an Act of Apostolical Power, such as was not to be a Precedent for the Church to follow in its Censures:

F   The

The quite contrary is the Truth, of which we have an undeniable Evidence, in the Dispute which *Tertullian* had with the Church in his time, for admitting Adulterers to Penance, who had this very Scripture alledged against him on behalf of the Church, that what was done was agreeable to the Precedent S. *Paul* had set the Church, in the case of this Incestuous Person at *Corinth* ; who being *put out of the Church* by S. *Paul's* Order in this place, was readmitted by his Indulgence, 2 *Cor.* 2. 7. How easie had it been for *Tertullian* to say, That there was nothing of Penance, nothing of Excommunication in this Act of S. *Paul's delivering* the Incestuous Person *to Satan*, or that what he did both in putting away, and in readmitting him to the Church, was an Act of Apostolical Authority, not to be a Precedent to the Church to do the like ? But this he could not say, knowing the Sense of the whole Church against him in it, and being himself satisfied that the Church would be justifiable in following the Example.

Tertullian *ae Pudicitia,* cap. 12, 13.

He therefore deviseth this Answer, That it is not the same case which is spoken of in both Epistles ; the Man put out of the Church by the Apostle's Order, 1 *Cor.* 5. was not the same that was readmitted and restored by his Indulgence, 2 *Cor.* 2. 7.

An

An answer plainly shewing his Sense, and that of the Church in his time to have been this, That it would be a sufficient justification of the Church's Proceedings, as well in passing its Censures, as in remitting them to have followed this Precedent of *S. Paul*; in what could be made appear to have been done by him in the present case. Which being so clear an Evidence of the Sense of the Primitive Church that nothing can be more, I may advance it here, as greatly for my purpose, to prove that I have rightly applied this Scripture, and have not been mistaken, neither in giving the Fact for an Instance of the *Power of the Keys*, nor in insisting upon the Act of *S. Paul*, to be a Precedent for the Church to act upon that Power in all times: The Primitive Church that best understood the Nature of Church Power, and the Effects of such Censures, making this a Precedent to it self, for what it did by Power from our Lord Jesus Christ, in the Censure of Offenders, and in the Relaxation of those Censures. And thus it appearing that the Primitive Church so thought of *S. Paul's* Act, as to make it a Precedent for it self; I need not allow it to be fit for me to dispute with the *Exposition*, whether the Primitive Church thought of *delivering to Satan* by its Cen-

sures.

fures.   For how could it think of following the Precedent, but by thinking to do
the fame thing ?   But perhaps I fhall have
it thrown overthwart me, that the Primitive Church muft then have thought of
fome vifible Punifhment by Evil Spirits,
enfuing upon its Cenfures, to fuch as
were thereby put out of the Church, becaufe this Effect followed on the Apoftle's
Cenfure.   But I can eafily get clear of
this Objection, by faying this which no
Man fhall eafily difprove, *viz.* That the
Primitive Church being neareft the time
of the Apoftles, knew beft, what in any of
their Acts was the Effect of *Miraculous
Power* and what not ; what the Difference
was between the Minifters of the Church
acting upon the Power of our Lord Jefus
Chrift, in the Things belonging to the
Church's Miniftry, and the Apoftles during the fame in their own Perfons : and
whatfoever extraordinary Effects appeared
in what the Apoftles acted thereupon, it
did not expect to follow upon the ordinary Minifters of the Church doing them :
but yet underftood at the fame time how
to make ufe of thofe extraordinary Effects
to confirm the Faith of the Church, that
God who had thus vifibly fhewn his Power
to be with the Church in what the Apoftles
did, was able to give Effect to the Acts of
his

his Church in the ordinary way, and would give them Effect accordingly. Had not the Primitive Church thus underftood to diftinguifh the Effects of *Extraordinary Power,* in Acts done by the Apoftles from the ordinary Miniftration, and the Effects following the fame ; I do not fee how the Church could have thought of retaining upon the Apoftles practice any, almoft of thofe things that have been retained, as ftanding Functions and Ordinances in the Church, fuch as *Impofition of Hands in Confirmation,* *Ordination* of Minifters, *Counfels* and Synods, even *Preaching* the Word and Baptifm it felf ; there being no one of thefe but what extraordinary Effects followed in the time of the Apoftles, efpecially when they performed any of them in their own Perfons: yet thofe the Church hath retained and pretendeth to follow the Apoftles in, with Confidence that the fame Spiritual Effects fhall follow to the Church in the ufe of them, as did in the Apoftles ufe thereof; thefe being neceffary for the Church to receive from God by fome means or other in all Times, and therefore to be expected in the ufe of thefe means which the Apoftles ufed on the behalf of God's Church to obtain them, and by which they were obtained through God's Grace and Goodnefs. Why then fhould it

Acts 19 5. & 6
2 Tim. 1. 6
Acts 15. 28.
Acts 10. 44
Acts 8. 15.

F 3 be

be imagined that the Primitive. Church thought not of the same Spiritual Effect from its Censure putting Scandalous Offenders out of the Church, which the Apostle had intimated to be the consequence of his doing it, the falling under the *Power* of *Satan* in a Spiritual Sense being the too sure Consequent of being put out of the Church of God at all times? And if there were nothing of this Evidence that I have been arguing from, I should rather take the Sense of the Primitive Church from what the *Homily* of our Church of *England* hath spoken of it, than from the Bishop of *Sarum's* Word alone. Now the speaking of Persons Excommunicate, saith thus, "They that were so justly Exempted *Homily* of the right Use of the Church, Part. 2. " and Banished, as it were from the House " of the Lord, were taken (as they be indeed) for Men divided and separated from " Christ's Church and in most dangerous " estate, yea, as St. *Paul* saith, even *given* " *unto Satan, the Devil for a time,* and " their Company was shunned and avoided " of all Godly Men and Women, until " such time as they by Repentance and " Publick Penance were Reconciled. So " *horrible a thing* was it to be *shut out of* " *the Church* and House of the Lord in " *those days* when Religion was most Pure, " and nothing so Corrupt as it hath been

of

" of late days. Where obferve alfo, the difference between the Opinion of the Bifhop
of *Sarum* (who offereth it as an Argument
that the Primitive Church meant not the
delivering to Satan by its Cenfure, That *it
thought nothing in this matter but of denying to fuffer Scandalous Perfons to mix with
the reft in the Sacrament, and in other parts
of the Worfhip,*) and the Senfe of the
Church of *England*, which reckoneth it
as an Effect of that Difcipline, (which
*would not fuffer open Offenders once to enter
into the Houfe of the Lord, nor to be admitted to Common-Prayer and the ufe of the Sacraments with other true Chriftians*) that
fuch Perfons by being excluded from the
Sacraments and the *other parts of Worfhip,*
were *even given unto Satan.* And *Tertullian* (who fhall be allowed to fpeak the
Senfe of the Primitive Church in what he
fpeaks of the general Practice thereof)
faith the fame in effect, when fpeaking of
the Exhortations, the Reproofs and Cenfures of the Church, (which were the
Methods of Primitive Difcipline,) He faith
*Summum futuri judicii præjudicium eft, fi-
quis ità deliquerit, ut à Communicatione O-
rationis & Conventûs & omnis Sancti commercii relegetur.* That if any one fo Offended as to be confined from *Prayers*, and
from the *Publick Affembly*, and debarred

Tertullian Apolog. Cap. 39.

from

from *all Communion in Holy Things,* The Judgment of the Church againſt ſuch an Offender was as the greateſt Judgment before-hand to the Judgment to come, that is to ſay, it was like a *Preſident* or *Ruled Caſe,* (which the word *Præjudicium* is many times uſed to ſignify.) to God's future Judgment for the excluding ſuch wicked ones from his Preſence, and from his Heavenly Kingdom. What could be ſaid more to expreſs the dangerous eſtate of ſuch as were ſhut out from the Houſe of God, and excluded the Aſſemblies for his Worſhip? And indeed by excluding from the Sacrament, and from the Aſſemblies for God's Worſhip, what can the Church at any time mean, but that the Perſons debarred from theſe, are barred from any Intereſt in God's Grace or Mercy, and being deſtitute of theſe, are they not really expoſed to *Satan,* who *goeth about as a Roaring Lion ſeeking whom he may Devour?* But the *Expoſition* ſays, " That the Primitive Church Admitted Sinners upon " the profeſſion of their Repentance, by an " Impoſition of Hands to ſhare in ſome " parts of the Worſhip, wherein they " ſtood by themſelves, and at a diſtance " from the reſt: And when they had paſſed " through ſeveral degrees in that ſtate of " Mourning, they were by ſteps received back

o

" back again to the Communion of the
" Church. And this (it faith) agrees
" well with the Nature and Ends of Church
" Power, which was given for *Edification,*
" and not for *Destruction,* and is suitable to
" the designs of the Gospel, for preserving
" the Society pure, and for reclaiming
" *those who* are otherwise like to be car-
" ried away by the *Devil in his Snare.*
This is a true Account, so far as it is an
Account of the Methods of Primitive Discipline, and a just Recognition of the sui-
tableness to the design, and of its efficacy to the Ends of Christianity. But the
Exposition hath herein only given us an
Account of the Church's dealing with
Penitents, that is to say, with those that
were admitted to Penance, and to the
Prayers of the Church for their Reconciliation with God. We are not told what the
Method was, that the Church took with
Refractory Sinners whom it could not
bring to Submit to the course of Penance,
nor with those that were guilty of so
gross Sins that the Church thought not fit
to admit them to the course of Penance
though they should desire it, until after
some time at least. Now these the Censure of the Church removed. *non modò à
limine, sed ab omni Ecclesiæ tecto,*as *Tertullian*'s Expression is, alluding to the several
stations

ſtations or places appointed for Penitents in the Church, whereas the *Excommunicate* were not allowed to come *within it.* Such were utterly excluded the Houſe of God, or the place of Aſſembly for his Worſhip, to denote their being put out of the Church of God ; *i. e.* from all Fellow-ſhip with his Saints and Servants, and from all part in the Intereſt which theſe have in God's Grace and Mercy.: that is, in effect they were delivered to *Satan,* thoſe who are deſtitute of God's Grace and Mercy, being under the Power of that Evil One that Ruleth in the Children of Diſobedience, and deceiveth them to go in the way of Wickedneſs, until they fall into Deſtruction. And indeed even this Act of Diſcipline, as it appertaineth to the *Au-*8 *thority which the Lord hath given to his Church,* ſo ſerveth it to the intent for which our Lord gave that Authority, *i. e.* for *Edification* and not for *Deſtruction.* The Apoſtle's Act in *delivering to Satan,* tho' underſtood to intend ſome immediate and viſible Puniſhment to him that was Ex-communicated by it, let it be even this, that as the Holy Ghoſt was poured out on all Chriſtians, ſo he that was thus put away from amongſt them ſhould be Poſ-ſeſſed or Haunted with an Evil Spirit, ne-vertheleſs had this intent in the *Deſtructi-*

on

on of the Flesh, or Punishment of the Body, that the *Spirit might be Saved in the Day of the Lord Jesus.* As the same is now under-stood by the Church to be a Spiritual Cen-sure, and used only to Spiritual Purposes, it cannot but be less liable (if rightly un-derstood) to the Objection of its not tend-ing to *Edification* but *Destruction.* It apparent-ly tendeth to the *Edification* of the Church in General, to the making and preserving it *a Glorious Church, Pure, Holy, and with-out Blemish,* to the *Building it up to be a Spi-ritual House,* an *Holy Priesthood* to *Offer up Spiritual Sacrifices acceptable to God by Jesus Christ,* whilst it putteth away that which *defileth,* every one that *worketh* wickedness and *Abomination* : Yea it designeth not the *Destruction* or *Damnation* of the Sinner whom it putteth out of the Church and delivereth to Satan, but that he may be Instructed to Repentance and Righteous-ness, and his Soul delivered out of the hands of that Enemy which would betray it to everlasting Destruction. Therefore is the vulgar prejudice against this Act of Discipline altogether unwarrantable, which because it is expressed by *delivering to Sa-tan,* esteemeth it unbecoming the Mini-sters of Christ, who should be concerned in the *Saving of Mens Souls,* but not in the *Damning of them.* Designing Men that have form'd this Prejudice in the Minds

of

1 Cor.

of simple Christians, must have conceal'd the truth, which is this, The Sins of such as this Act of Discipline putteth out of the Church hath first brought them into the Snare of the Devil and subjected them to his Power, before the Church *judgeth* to put away and *deliver them to Satan;* and this the Church also judgeth with intent to Rescue them as a Prey out of the Teeth of the Dragon that devoureth Souls; it putteth them into imminent danger, not that they should be swallowed up in *it,* but that they may become sensible of their dangerous estate, and that the apprehensions of Terror and a fearful looking for of Judgment *might warn them to flee from the Wrath to come,* whilst there is yet some possibility of their Escape through God's extraordinary Mercy, if they will fly to that Refuge.

I should not have dwelt so long upon this Argument, but that I proposed some advantages to my purpose from it, which I think my self to have also gained; namely, an Evidence of the Apostles taking Order with the Churches of their Planting, for the Exercise of that Power which Christ gave to his Church for the Government thereof in Righteousness, and for the Establishment of a Discipline therein for this purpose, which the reference of
this

this Scripture to fome fuch Order that muft have been taken by St. *Paul* with the Church of *Corinth*, hath cleared: The Senfe alfo of the Primitive Church un-derftanding this Scripture as by me it is underftood, to afford an Inftance of the *Power of the Keys,* and to yield a Prece-dent to the Church to Act upon this Pow-er in all times: Likewife a Proof that the Apoftle's Act of *delivering to Satan* was (fetting afide what extraordinary Effect might happen, if it pleafed God to fhew his Power with his Church in fome vifible Punifhment) no other than the *Putting out of the Church;* from which, whofoever was put away, fell into Satan's Power, in-to the Snare of the Deceiver, and into the Power of the Deftroyer of Souls. And as by delivering to Satan is meant (as fhall be fhewn) the *Putting out of the Church,* of which no doubt can remain to him that as a Chriftian hath reafon to think, that whofoever is not in the Church is in the Power of Satan, hereby is it gained, that another Paffage of Scripture, 1 *Tim.* 1.20. Where St. *Paul* faith that he had delivered *Hymenæus* and *Philetus unto Satan, that they might learn not to Blafpheme,* fhall be alfo underftood to be another Inftance of the Apoftle's Acting upon the *Power of the Keys,* and to imply a Difcipline in the
Churches

Churches of his Planting; For whereſoever this laſt degree of Cenſure appeareth, it ſhall infer the other methods of Diſcipline that appear in the Practice of the Church to have been in uſe alſo, and that this Cenſure came to paſs, becauſe either the milder methods could not work upon the Obſtinacy of the Offender, or the Crime was ſuch, that a leſs Cenſure was not thought ſufficient to give Conviction to the Sinner of his Guilt and Danger. And for the like Reaſon, if any Inſtances may be found in Scripture of *Admonition, Reproof,* or *Cenſure,* not reaching ſo far as Excommunication, as thoſe ſhall be an Argument that there was a courſe taken for Diſcipline in the Church, where ſuch Acts or Directions relating to ſuch Acts appear, ſo ſhall it be ſuppoſed that where theſe could not work the Reformation of Sinners, there ſhould follow that utmoſt Judgment and Cenſure which the Church had Power from Chriſt to Paſs and Execute. We are not to expect, as I have ſaid, for a Reaſon already given, (that is to ſay, the Epiſtles to the Churches being written by the Apoſtles on particular occaſions) to find an account therein at large of the Order taken with thoſe Churches concerning Diſcipline, but only occaſional hints and intimations of that which was done, or ought to be done:

done : But thefe being put together and appearing to be the fame with what is found in the Practice of the Primitive Church or in Rules which that acknowledged, the likenefs and agreement between them fhall be a good prefumption as that the whole was from the Apoftles, fo that in thefe Churches of their Planting, where inftances or directions appear of or concerning any Parts of Difcipline, there fome Order was taken by them for fuch Difcipline as we fee to have been in the Primitive Church. If any Man approve not this Argument, it will lie upon him to give fome account, how the Apoftles came to do the very fame things which a Power was fuppofed to be given for, in the *Power of the Keys*, given by Chrift to his Church for the Remitting and Retaining Sins, unlefs they underftood the Authority given by our Saviour therein to fuch purpofes: How the Writings of the Apoftles that are not Intelligible otherwife, fhould be fo eafily intelligible when underftood to fpeak of thofe things that were Practifed in the Primitive Difcipline, but that indeed they refer to fome Order taken with the Church for fuch a Difcipline : Or how the Practice of the Primitive Church fhould come to be the fame with that which we have intimations of

in

in the Writings of the Apostles, if both were not from their Authority: And how the same Customs and Rules in this matter should have taken place throughout the whole Church, if all Churches had not understood themselves to have a Power from Christ and his Apostles for this Purpose, and that the Church by the Ministry entrusted with it, was obliged to imploy *Exhortations, Reproofs* and *Censures,* (which were the universal Practice of the Church) for the purpose of bringing Sinners to acknowledge their faults, and to go through a course of Repentance; and to adjudge to a farther Censure for putting out of the Church, where either these could not prevail on the obstinacy of the Sinner, or where the Crime was such as was not to be allowed hope of forgiveness by the Church; Until therefore some other Account be given of this, more Probable and more Rational, which I do not expect to see; this Act also of S. *Paul's delivering* to *Satan Hymenæus* and *Alexander,* that is, putting them out of the Church, shall be deemed to be an Act done upon the *Power of the Keys,* and to imply a Discipline in the Church wherein he did it, as also to be a Precedent for the Church to do the like in case of others that should make *Shipwreck of the Faith,*

and

and *put away a good Conscience as those had* done; whom therefore he delivered unto *Satan,* to the end that they might *learn not to Blaspheme,* which, whether it signify not to speak Evil of the Truth, as is usual with such as have departed from the Faith, that they may not seem to have done it without cause; or that they should not give occasion for the Name of God to be Blasphemed by the Sins they lived in, having put away a good Conscience; or not to speak Evil of, and despise that Authority that reproved their Wickedness, and would have reclaimed them by gentle methods, if it had been possible: It shall be meant that the Apostle passed this Censure on them, that they might be Disciplined or Instructed by this Act of Discipline to reform and recover from that Sin which caused their being put out of the Church. So that in this Instance also the End of this Censure appeareth to have been not the Destruction of the Sinner, but his Reformation and Repentance to the saving of his Soul: that is, This was the End, supposing the Person under this Censure to regard the same, and to Repent accordingly; but indeed supposing him not to Repent, he continued in the Power of Satan to which that Censure delivered him which put him out of the Church, and

G what

what the consequence of that must be
as to the state of such a Man's Soul I need
not say; for the Mind of every Man that
hath been once instructed in the knowledge of a Christian, doth surely forebode
the Evil to come.

But I come again to the Business between S. *Paul* and the *Corinthians,* when he
comes to advise them to *restore* to the *Communion* of the Church the Person, whom he
had before, as we have seen, required them
to *put away* from among them, 2. *Cor.*
2. 6. His Words are these. *Sufficient to
such a Man is this Punishment which was inflicted of many; so that contrariwise, ye ought
rather to forgive him and comfort him, lest
perhaps such a one should be Swallowed up
with overmuch Sorrow.* Wherefore *I beseech
you that you would confirm your Love towards him. For to this end also did I write,
that I might know the proof of you, whether
ye be obedient in all things. To whom ye forgive any thing, I forgive also; for if I forgave any thing, To whom I forgave it, for
your sakes forgave I it* in the Person of
Christ; *lest Satan should get an advantage
over us; for we are not ignorant of his devices.* I said before that *Tertullian* was of
Opinion that it was not the same Man
whom the Apostle commanded them to deliver to Satan in his first Epistle, and in
whose

whofe favour he writes fo much in his
Second: But as the whole Church was
againft *Tertullian* in this his Opinion, and
in that which drove him to be of this
Opinion, Namely, his not believing that
the Apoftle would, or that the Church
therefore could admit fuch a Sinner upon
any Penance; fo likewife is this Opinion
of his excluded by the exprefs Words of
the Scripture. *For to this end alfo did I
write to know the proof of you*, which fhew
that this is the Cafe that he Writ of in
his former Epiftle. The Cafe therefore
was this: Upon S. *Paul*'s firft Epiftle
he was delivered to Satan, The Church
of *Corinth* being obedient to, and executing his Order, did that which the Apoftle had blamed them for not doing afore,
1 *Cor.* 5. 2. The Cenfure being Executed has this Effect, that the Proud Offender is become Humble, Sorrowful, and
Penitent, feeks to the Church, that had
Cenfured him, to be Receiv'd again among
them; but thofe who acted on the Church's
behalf not being forward to grant him
admittance, becaufe they had incurred
blame for not doing their Duty in the Cenfure of him at the firft, he prevails with
fome of them however to fend to S. *Paul*
on his behalf, and to let him know
his Sorrow and Repentance, which feems

to have given the Apostle occasion to write
to the Church of *Corinth* in his favour,
that himself was content, upon the Submission of the Offender, and upon the Report of such as had proposed to him to
be satisfied with the Censure that had been,
and with the Sorrow wrought thereby in
him that had committed the Fault, to
take off the Censure which he therefore
willeth the Church also to take off, that
he who had been so *put away from among
them,* might be restored to their *Communion* and *Fellowship.* That this was the
Case, the matter he writes plainly show-
eth, for when he saith, *sufficient for such
a one is the Censure inflicted by many ;* what
is the Censure inflicted by many ? But
the Censure which the Church, upon
S. *Paul's* Order had passed in the Case, in
which the whole Church had agreed, being prevail'd with by what he had written
in his first Epistle to do their Duty, and
to put away from among them that wicked Person: And what meaneth his say-
ing *Sufficient is the Censure ?* but this, That
the Censure having passed, and having also had its Effect, it was enough, and
there was no necessity of continuing the
Offender under it, It might be taken off.
When therefore he saith, *so that contrariwise ye ought to forgive him, and comfort
him ;*

him ; what is it but this, that they ought to take it off, the Offender's Sorrow and Repentance having appeared ? and this for fear of an Evil on the other side , *lest perhaps such a one should be swallowed up with overmuch Sorrow* , that is , lest he should be out of all hope, and fall into despair of God's Mercy, if the Church would not remit the Censure, and admit him to some hope thereof through their Prayers. What is it that he saith again, that *he writ to them before for this end, to see whether they would be obedient in all things ?* But this, that tho he wrote to them to do their Duty, and put away from them that wicked Person, and he liked well that they had been obedient to him and done it, yet it was not his meaning that the Censure should not be taken off again, having had its effect, to work Sorrow and Repentance in the Sinner; but that as he wrote that they should do their duty in putting away, so it would please him well that they should ; yea, he entreateth them that they would now restore him again to their Communion, and thereby *confirm their Love towards him*, so as that he might be perswaded by their readiness to receive him upon his Repentance, that even their Censure of him proceeded from Love towards him, from pure Kindness and Love to his

Soul,

G 3

Soul, that this *might be saved in the day of the Lord Jesus.* And when he faith, *To whom ye forgive any thing, I forgive also ; for if I forgave any thing, for your sakes forgave I it to him that I did forgive it, in the Person of Christ ;* was it not to let them know that had proposed to him to be content with the Censure that had been passed, and to consent to its being remitted, since the Penitence of the Sinner appeared ; that he was content to agree thereto, and as willing that the Censure should be now taken off as they were? And to let the rest of the Church, who waited to hear from him in the case, know that he had for his own part taken it off by the same Authority that he had first enjoyned them to Pass the Censure, that they therefore were now as much concerned to take it off as they were before to pass it, if they would approve themselves as they had already in this Matter, *obedient to him in all things;* which that they might be more willing unto, he assures them that it was *for their sakes* that he was now ready to remit the Censure which he had before required them to lay on; To the end that their Censure might have the Effect, which as Christians they must have proposed from it, whereas that Effect otherwise might be obstructed in the circum-

stances

ftances the Penitent was, who being now humbled, defired and fought it with Tears. And to the end also that there might be no. Faction nor Divifion among them, whilft fome might be for admitting him and others not. Both which things the Apoftle feems to have feared, and to have been defirous to prevent, and in that re-fpect to have faid, *left Satan fhould get advantage of us, for we are not ignorant of his Devices.* Wherein he muft mean, ei-ther that Satan might get fome advantage in refpect of the Perfon Excluded, which what could it be but by his Tempting him, either to defpair of his Salvation, or to defpife the Authority of the Church? Either of which muft fruftrate the Effect of the Church's Cenfure, or that Satan might get fome advantage over the Church that had paffed the Cenfure, and this in what more likely than in dividing them upon it? This therefore the Apoftle would have them agree with him to pre-vent, by Re-admitting the Offender upon his Repentance, to the Communion of the Church. But here, to fpeak my own thoughts, there feems to be a miftake in this, that 'tis commonly thought, that St. *Paul* here re-admits the Offender to the *Communion* of the Church; whereas he ra-ther feems to admit him only to Penance

and

and to the *Prayers of the Church.* My Reason is, because the strictness of Discipline under the Apostles will hardly allow that such an Offender should be forthwith readmitted to the Communion of the Church, but to a course of Penance, in order to obtain Reconcilement with God, and to hopes of God's Mercy when this course of Repentance should be gone through. The Censure that passed upon him seems to have been such as so excluded him from the Church, that he was not allowed the means of Reconciliation with God by the Warrant of the Church, tho' not excluded from the hope of it by the Mercy of God. This his having no comfort from the Church made him so near being *swallowed up with Sorrow* ; he being so excluded as to be denied the means of Reconcilement by the Church seems also to be that from whence Satan might have advantage to drive him to Despair, which might produce Apostacy or some other very great Evil. To one in these circumstances it must be a great comfort to have the Censure that was against him, so far abated as to be admitted to a course of Penance and to the Prayers of God's Church towards his Reconcilement: In this the Church must have given sufficient cause to think their Censure proceeded from *Love towards him.*

him, from a true concern and care for his Soul, whilst there was an endeavour to instruct him to Repentance, such as might be to *Salvation, not to be Repented of.* This was enough to prevent his being *swallow'd up with overmuch Sorrow,* there being hope given of his Reconcilement with God sufficient to keep him from Despair, when the Church should take upon it to instruct him to Repentance, and Offer Prayers to God on his behalf for, his obtaining God's Peace and Pardon. In admitting him also to this, S. *Paul* and the Church may be said to forgive, and this *in the Person of Christ,* that is, by Authority from him, as by admitting him to Penance they allowed him hope of God's Forgiveness, and of the Church's Warrant thereof at the end of that course of Repentance, as hereby he was instructed in the right and sure way of obtaining forgiveness, and assisted with their Prayers towards it. But whatsoever become of this Opinion of mine in the matter, which I own the strictness of Discipline under the Apostles, and in the Primitive Church after them (not soon, nor easily admitting Persons guilty of Crimes of this nature to the Communion of the Church) to have given occasion for: whether you will think with me, that the Favour S. *Paul* shew'd, was the abatement

ment of the Censure, and admitting the Offender to Penance, in order to his being restored to the Communion of the Church when that should be performed, and a grant of the Prayers of the Church towards the means of his Reconcilement; or with others, that it was a full Release of the Censure, whereby he that was put away from the Church, was now fully restored to the Communion thereof; in either case there will appear such evident marks and tokens of the Discipline of Penance, and of Power in the Church to exercise such a Discipline; yea, of an Obligation upon the Church to imploy its Ministry accordingly, that wilful Prejudice must shut our Eyes, if we see them not. The Favour or Indulgence granted presupposeth the Censure which it mitigateth, and therefore the Communion of the Church either abated, or quite taken from him whom it restoreth to it. It could not have been said *sufficient to such a one is the Censure inflicted of many,* had it not been that the Church had put him under Censure. Nor would this have been said by the Apostle to be *sufficient,* but that the Censure had its Effect to make him *sorrowful to Repentance.* When he saith, that *contrariwise* now they *ought* rather *to forgive*

give *him and comfort him ,* left *perhaps fuch* a one *fhould be fwallowed up with overmuch* forrow, it fuppofeth the Cenfure to have diminifhed, if not taken away from him his hope of God's Mercy, in that the Church would not allow him fhare in the common intreft that Chriftians may have therein, and the fad Profpect of his Cir-cumftances to have brought him fo near the being *fwallowed up with forrow :* It di-recteth likewife the Church of God what is to be done, when an Offender becomes humble and penitent upon its Cenfure, that then the Cenfure is to be abated, and the Penitent admitted to the Comfort of the Prayers of his Fellow-Chriftians: or fuppofing the Sorrow fuch as hath wrought the Converfion of the Sinner, then is it to be taken off and wholly releafed, and the Communion of the Church to be granted him in affurance of God's Mercy and Pardon. When the Apoftle faith, he *forgave in the Perfon of Chrift,* and alfo telleth the Church that they ought to for-give and comfort the forrowful Perfon ; as this Act of his and of the Church muft be refolved into the Power of Binding and Loofing, of Retaining and Remitting Sins given by our Lord in the Gofpel under the Symbole of the Keys of his Houfe, fo it intimateth alfo to us wherein that Power con-

confisteth, and how far it extendeth, namely, That the Ministers of Christ's Church by this Commission are Authorized to give Forgiveness of Sins to whomsoever they shall find disposed by serious Contrition and true Sorrow of Heart to receive it at God's Hands ; and this not only so as to *Declare* it, but *Authoritatively to assure* it ; otherwise, how should what the Church did in Forgiving, be matter of such *Comfort* to the Penitent ? Or its refusal to Forgive, be the occasion of his being *Swallowed up with overmuch Sorrow* ? The Reason must be this, that he could not assure himself so well of God's Forgiveness, as the Church might assure him thereof, should that judge his Repentance sincere, or take upon it to set him in a way for the perfecting of his Repentance; and his Hope would be the greater when the Church should give him the assistance of the Prayers thereof towards his Reconcilement with God. Yet this may not be understood to intimate that the Power of the Keys, by which Sins are Bound or Remitted, is such, as that Pronouncing Sentence of Forgiveness, God shall Ratify it, or, that Binding or Retaining shall bear no hope of any kind, as to God's Mercy; for we may be assured, that God gives Pardon to whomsoever he sees disposed to

receive

receive it, and that difpofition indeed being once brought to pafs, the Miniftry of the Keys confifteth only in declaring the Pardon given by God. Neverthelefs the Miniftry of the Keys acteth in bringing that difpofition to pafs, in procuring that difpofition of the heart, which is requifite to make Men capable of Forgivenefs, in bringing them to the knowledge of their Sins, in directing the courfe which they have to take in feeking their Reconcilement with God, in judging alfo concerning the Repentance wrought, and affuring God's Forgivenefs upon the beft judgment that it can make of the difpofition it hath laboured to procure, and fo far as the Prayers of the Church on the Penitent's behalf can add to the confidence of his being heard in what he asketh of God, as to his Pardon and Reconcilement. In which refpect the Church forgiving affordeth not a little Comfort to a Penitent; as on the contrary, this retaining his Sins doth it to his forrow, and to the increafing of his fears in refpect of God's Judgment. When St *Paul* faith that he *forgave*, and would have them to *forgive*, left *Satan fhould get an advantage of them, of whfe devices they were not ignorant*; if this be underftood in refpect to the Party excluded, the meaning is, as I have

have said before, left Satan should take advantage otherwise to drive him to despair, or tempt him to despise the Authority of the Church either of which must frustrate the Church's Censure, as to its doing any good upon the Offender, towards the saving of his Soul : This first therefore intimateth to us that the design of the Church's Censure, which had passed for the *delivery of such a one to Satan*, was, as hath been said before, that his being delivered to Satan might make way for his escape out of the Snare, and getting clear from the Power of the Devil; which S. *Chrysostom* taking notice of, observes upon the Place as I remember, somewhere to this purpose, That the Person was not said to be *given* to Satan, but only *delivered*; a distinction, that if it have not ground in the Words, it has in the Thing, in the nature of the Sentence, and the End declared by the Apostle before, when he saith it was for the *saving of the Soul in the Day of the Lord Jesus*, (which could not be if the delivering to Satan had been the giving into his Power to hold and keep): which end the Apostle sheweth himself to have always sought in this, that he presseth the Church to take off the Censure, left *Satan should* otherwise *get advantage*; whose getting advantage over the Person excluded, he would not have

have been folicitous to prevent, had he been before delivered to Satan for the purpofe of his having advantage over him, and taking him into his Power and Poffeffion. This moreover intimateth what fhould be the Church's aim in all times in its miniftration of Difcipline, as well when it putteth under Cenfure as when it releafeth from fuch Cenfures, namely, the prevention of Satan's getting advantage to Ruin thofe Souls which the Church is concerned to feek to Save. This Aim being purfued, juftifieth that difference which may be obferved to have been in the way of Penance and Reconcilement in the Church, which hath fometimes been moft ftrict in its Difcipline, not admitting fome fort of Sins to any Penance, or at leaft, not till the point of Death, or till after a long time ; and at other times hath abated much of that Rigour ; and this is as well according to the Circumftances of the Church, as according to the figns of Repentance appearing in the Offender. As to the Senfe of the Church, underftanding this Scripture to be good Evidence for a Difcipline in the Church to Cenfure Offenders, and put them out of the Church, if they will not otherwife be brought to Repentance, and to abate of fuch Cenfure, or take it off when the Sinner fhall become

Humble

Humble and Penitent; I shall not alledg
what has been Argued to this Purpose from
it by Papists, and not Deny'd by Prote-
stants since *Luther* first Disputed against Indulgences, but rather, the use which the
Church made thereof heretofore against
the *Montanists* and *Novatians,* urging the
Example of S. *Paul* in this Place to be E-
vidence for a Power in the Church, to
abate or take off its Censures as that shou'd
see cause, from the Submission or Repentance of them, that for the Crimes of A-
dultery or Apostacy were excluded the
Church: For though *Tertullian,* as a *Mon-
tanist,* reply that it was not the same Person, who for Incest, a Crime as great or
greater than Adultery, had been put out of
the Church by S. *Paul*'s Order, that is here
Restored; yet he does not deny this to
be some Favour and Indulgence to some
Person that was under Censure for some
less Crime; so that of all hands it has
been agreed to refer to a Discipline in the
Church, that could put under Censure
such as Professing themselves Christians,
should live in Sins, inconsistent with that
Profession, and might in most cases at least,
if not in all, when such Offenders should
be humbled, admit them to Penance, and
by degrees Receive them again into the
Communion of the Church, and so restore
them

them to the hope of God's Mercy and Pardon, which that Communion supposeth and assureth.

There is yet another Passage in this Epistle of *S. Paul* to the *Corinthians; 2 Cor. 12. 20.* that seems to speak plainly of a Discipline that *S. Paul* intended to make use of, for the Correcting Faults that some among them were guilty of, *I fear* (saith he) *left when I come, I shall not find you such as I would, and that I shall be found unto you such as ye would not ; left there be* Debates, Envyings, Wrath, Strifes, Back-bitings, Whisperings, Swellings, Tumults : *And left when I come again, my God will humble me among you, and that I shall bewail many which have Sinned already, and have not Repented of the Uncleannefs, and Fornication, and Lasciviousnefs which they have committed.* What is this that he *feareth that he should not find them such as he would,* but that he was afraid he should not find them so good Christians as he would have them to be? And again, that he should *be found of them, such as they would not,* but in respect of the Resolution he had taken to Rebuke and Censure their Faults? he not intending any longer to bear with their *Debates, Envyings, Wrath, Strifes,* and other unchristian Practices and Behaviour, altogether unbecoming their holy Profession. And this

H that

that he said he was afraid of, *left God ſhould humble him among them when he came,* and that he ſhould *Mourn for many that had Sinned afore, and not Repented* (by that time he ſhould come) *of the Uncleanneſs, Whoredom, and Wantcnneſs which they had done,* but that he feared he ſhould, to his Sorrow, be under a neceſſity of Puniſhing and Cenſuring the Faults of ſuch as ſhould not ſhew themſelves to have Repented of ſuch their Faults before his coming? This is S. *Chryſoſtom*'s Expoſition of this Scripture, that when he ſpeaks of *mourning* for many, it is in reſpect of the *Sorrow* that it would be to him to be under a *neceſſity of Puniſhing them,* and that he ſpeaketh thus to give them warning that they might Repent them of thoſe their Faults, and that ſuch as ſhould not, he would treat at his coming as Perſons under an incurable *Diſeaſe,* who are given over and their Cure deſpaired of. But a greater Authority than this of S. *Chryſoſtom*'s is that of the Apoſtle himſelf, who finding fault with the *Corinthians* in his former Epiſtle, that they had not *mourned to put away him that had done Evil,* muſt reaſonably be ſuppoſed to mean the ſame thing when here he ſpeaks of *mourning* himſelf, in reſpect of *many that had Sinned and ſhould not have Repented* before

his

his coming. It being evident also by divers Passages in Ancient Christian Authors, that Excommunication in the Primitive Church was Solemnized in a Fashion of Mourning, as for a Member lost; and likewise that a Sorrow was expressed by the Church on the Penitent's behalf when he was admitted to Penance, and Prayers were made for his Reconcilement to God ; this will justify beyond all exception the reason of this Mourning of S. *Paul,* to be for those whom he should be constrained to put out of the Church for Sins which they had committed, and not shewn any Repentance for. Besides there is something cometh after, which makes this appear to be his meaning yet more plainly, and that is the Severity which he threatneth against the Obstinate Sinners, 2 *Cor.* 13..2. Saying, *Now I write to them which heretofore have Sinned, and to all others, that if I come again I will not spare,* and more to the same purpose, Verse 10. *Therefore I write these things being absent, left being present I should use sharpness, according to the Power which the Lord hath given me, to Edification, and not to Destruction.* What is this that he would not *spare them that had Sinned,* but that he would not spare sharply to Rebuke them, or rather, (he having done this already by this his Epistle) to Pu-

H 2   nish

nifh them fo far as his Power in Chrift
would reach to do it? For what elfe is
that which he would not willingly be forced to, the *ufing fharpnefs according to the
Power which the Lord had given him,* but
the Extremity of Cenfure, which by Power from Chrift he might, and fhould be
obliged to ufe againft fuch Sinners if
they continued Obftinate, and would not
take notice of, and warning from this
which he tells them, of his Power to Cenfure fuch Offences, and of his purpofe
to make ufe of that Power, yea, of his
being under a neceffity to ufe it againft
them that fhould not repent them of their
wickednefs? What this *Power* was which
the *Lord had given him,* and which he
purpofed to ufe againft them he doth not
fay: He declares indeed that the Lord
had given it him, to *Edification,* and not to
Deftruction, and therein intimates his purpofe to ufe it accordingly, that they might
reft affur'd that even the *fharpnefs* he fhou'd
ufe, fhould be for the good of their Souls,
notwithftanding whatfoever Severity he
might be conftrained to proceed againft
them with. And as for the *Power,* whatever it was, he was refolved to ufe it a-
gainft *them that had Sinned, and had not
Repented ;* It may reafonably be prefumed
therefore to be fome Power of his Miniftry,

ſtry, which, whoever will not think to be the
ſame with that which Chriſt gave to his
Church and Diſciples, for Binding and
Looſing, and Remitting and Retaining Sins,
ought to ſhew what other Power it was, and
when given him by the Lord. In the mean
time, I cannot but reſt fully perſwaded,
that Chriſt our Saviour being known to
have given a Power to his Church under
the Symbole of the Keys of his Houſe, for
the Removing and Putting out of the
Church Scandalous Sinners, when his A-
poſtle threatens to make uſe of a Power
which he hath from Chriſt againſt ſuch as
have Sinned and not Repented, he muſt mean
a Power, which they, as Chriſtians, muſt
underſtand him to have as part of his Miniſtry entruſted with him by Chriſt our Lord;
which therefore having in Truſt, he might
well write to them as though he were under a neceſſity, and kind of compulſion
to uſe it againſt them that ſhould not *Repent* before his coming; they themſelves
being ſenſible that his Truſt, as to that
Power which the Lord had given him could
not be diſcharged otherwiſe, if no other
means could prevail with them. He that
will, however, is free for me, to ſuppoſe ſome
extraordinary Effect of this *Power* in S. *Paul*,
which the Sentence of Excommunication
in theſe days produceth not; for I have

H 3   allowed

allowed, that during the time of the Apoftles, to manifeſt God's Preſence in his
Church; thoſe that were ſhut out of it,
became ſubject to viſible Evils and Plagues,
which S. *Paul* might mean, when he ſpeaketh of the *Deſtruction of Fleſh,* intimating
ſome Puniſhment of the Body, to Reduce
the Spirit to a fear of God's future Judgment, that ſo it might inwardly reſolve
upon that Repentance, which through
Chriſt ſaveth from the Wrath to come.
Nevertheleſs, this being a Thing conſe-
quent on the Cenſure that then ſhut ſuch
Perſons out of the Church, this of putting out of the Church ſhall be preſumed
to be the Power that S. *Paul* would not
ſpare to uſe againſt them that had Sinned,
and not Repented of their Wickedneſs.

But to go farther, There is a Paſſage in
S. *Paul's* Epiſtle to the *Galatians,* that
ſeemeth plainly to imply, and refer to ſome
Order taken with that Church alſo, for a
Diſcipline therein, *Gal. 6. 1. Brethren,
if a Man be overtaken in a Fault, ye which
are Spiritual, reſtore ſuch a one in the Spirit
of Meekneſs, conſidering thy ſelf, leſt thou
alſo be tempted.* Here he ſuppoſeth it the
Duty of thoſe that were endued with *Spiritual* Gifts and Graces (as eſpecially they
that had the Rule of the Church of Chriſt
were) to *reſtore* ſuch of their Chriſtian
                                Brethren

Brethren as fhould be *overtaken* in any fault, doing things unbecoming and inconfiftent with their Chriftian Profeffion. How fhould they underftand they were to *reftore* fuch, but by putting them upon Repentance; And how fhould they do this without fome Authority or Power to conftrain them thereunto? who being alfo bidden to go about this with *meeknefs*; it is to be fuppofed that they had fome Authority over fuch Delinquents, which they fhould ufe with Moderation and Mildnefs, yea and Compaffion; confidering themfelves to be Men of like Paffions and Infirmities, and liable to like Temptations. I am not moved to think this to be any thing of another nature; becaufe the Apoftle directs himfelf here to the whole Church, and not particularly to thofe that had the Miniftery therein, becaufe all the People had an intreft in what was done by the Church, as to the cenfuring of Offenders, or reproving their Faults, fuch Reproofs and Cenfures always paffing at their Publick Affemblies, wherein neverthelefs fuch particular Perfons acted always for the Body, as were authorized by their Miniftry for that purpofe.

There is moreover a Paffage in one of S. *Paul's* Epiftles to the *Theffalonians*, which feems to be an Order taken for a Difci-

H 4 pline

pline in that Church also ; yea a Command relating to it, enjoined in the Name of our Lord Jesus Christ, which therefore being grounded upon his Authority, all Christians shall be obliged to regard and fulfil. It is in 2 *Theff.* 3. 6. *Now we command you, Brethren, that ye withdraw your selves from every Brother that walketh disorderly, and not after the Tradition which he received of us.* And *ver.* 14. *If any Man obey not our Word by this Epistle, note that Man, and have no company with him, that he may be ashamed.* What is it that they should *withdraw themselves from the disorderly;* but the same with that which he giveth in charge in his Epistle to the *Romans, cap.* 16. 17. that they should *mark them which cause divisions and offences, contrary to the Doctrine which they had learned; and avoid them?* Which by the way, I observe to be an Instance of some Order in that Church of *Rome,* also to the like purpose. Now *withdrawing from, avoiding and not keeping company with,* seem all one and the same, importing the not having any Fellowship or Society with such; whom if they were to avoid, so as not to have any Civil Conversation with them, much more so as not to have communion with them in Holy Things. A like Order the Apostle giveth, 1 *Cor.* 5. 11.

(whereof

(whereof fome notice has been taken already) *not to keep company, if any Man that is called a Brother be a Fornicator, or Covetous, or an Idolater, or a Railer, or a Drunkard, or an Extortioner, with fuch an one, no not to eat.* This may be good Counfel only if the Apoftle be thought to direct himfelf to Particular Chriftians only ; but as he writes unto the *Church of the Theffalonians,* or to any other Church in general Terms to *withdraw from, avoid and not company* with fuch Perfons, it is to be fuppofed that Church fhould underftand it felf obliged to *note, mark,* and feparate fuch from the Society and Communion of Chriftians, and that Private Chriftians fhould apprehend it their concern, to take notice of fuch as are thus condemned by the Church, to *avoid them,* and not to have any familiarity with them, *not fo much as to eat* with them ; to demonftrate how far they would be from communicating with them in the Offices of Chriftianity. Otherwife we muft fuppofe S. *Paul* to have ufed a very weak Argument to the *Corinthians,* when he gives this for a Reafon why they were to blame, for that they had not *put away from among them* the Inceftuous Perfon, becaufe he had *wrote unto them in an Epiftle, not to company with Fornicators,* 1 Cor. 5. 9. were it not that they might

might easily thence have underftood, that if they were not to hold Civil Converfe and Society with fuch, much lefs fhould they have fuffered fuch to have continued in Communion with the Church ; from which, they well knew, they had a Power from Chrift to exclude them and put them away. And otherwife, alfo, how fhould this be good Reafoning. in the Apoftle, when he faith he did not mean to require them to forbear the company of the *Gentiles* in fuch cafe ; but that they fhould not keep company with a *Brother* being a Fornicator, &c. For that neither he nor they had *to do to judge thofe that are without*, whom they muft therefore leave to God's Judgment ; but they had Power to judge thofe that were of the Church or *within*, and therefore having this Power, they could not but apprehend, that if he forbid them to company with fuch, it was their duty as a Church *to put away* from among themfelves every fuch wicked Perfon ; and with thofe that fhould be fo put away, no Chriftian might keep company *fo much as to eat.* Let it be obferved here alfo; that this Interpretation is not mine ; but what the practice of the whole Church inforceth, wherein the Company of Perfons Excommunicate was ever fhunned and avoided, by faithful Chriftians, until fuch time

time as they were admitted to Penance, in order to their being reconciled and received into the Church.

Moreover, the Order taken for the excluding of Hereticks out of the Church, as that of S. *Paul,* Gal. 1. 9. *If any Man preach any other Gospel than that ye have received, let him be Anathema;* that is, as the Antients have interpreted it, Let him be separated, set aside, shut out of the Church, to expect his Judgment at the coming of Christ: And *Tit.* 3. 9. *A Man that is an Heretick after the first and second admonition reject* with others of like nature: as it importeth the Power of the Keys, to exclude from the Church such as depart from the Truth; therein is it an Evidence of that Authority which bringeth to Effect the Discipline thereof, by excluding those that will not be otherwise perswaded, but to hold the Truth in unrighteousness. The Power that excludeth is the same, how different soever the Causes of exclusion may be, and the Instances in every case, as they are alike Evidences of the Church's Power, shall help to justifie the use of such a Power, in every case that the Reason of Christianity will warrant. Indeed if I might be allowed to offer at a conjecture, touching the Reason of S. *Paul*'s directing this

Power

Power of the Church to be imployed a-
gainſt Hereticks that deny ſome Truth or
other of Chriſtianity ; I ſhould be apt to
ſay, that probably 'twas becauſe all Chriſtian Truth was depoſited with the Church
to be a Foundation for its being built up,
and edified in Righteouſneſs ; ſo that the
oppoſing of the Truth is a weakning of
the Foundation of Godlineſs, and either
hinders the Practice thereof, or takes from
the obligations that all are under to that
Practice ; and the Errors that Hereticks
ſubſtitute in the room of Chriſtian Truth,
are wicked Principles, that will produce
wicked practices ; which practices, though
ſome that hold Heretical Errors may diſown, or may not be guilty of (the Truth,
which they hold, probably prevailing over
the Poiſon of their Errors, that the Infection does not ſo corrupt their Manners
as otherwiſe it would) yet in as much as
ſuch Errors tend to wickedneſs, or give
advantage to Sinners to do wickedly, this
ſhall be Reaſon ſufficient for the Church
to imploy its Authority againſt ſuch Hereticks, to cut off thereby the Sourſe of
Wickedneſs, and to prevent Sinners of
any advantage they may think to make of
ſuch Hereſies, to proceed in their Evil
Works.   But this is conjecture only, that
Hereſie and Hereticks were detected ſo as
that

that was condemned, and thefe were cut off from the Church, upon the account that Hereticks were wicked, and their Herefie made them wicked in their Practices and Lives: If it were for another Caufe that had not refpect to this, and they were put out of the Church, barely for profeffing to believe the contrary of that which they profefled, when they were made Chriftians; Shall it not be as reafonable that the Church put away alfo thofe, who having made Profeffion of a Chriftian Life, in their Works and Practices deny it, and depart from it, being Vile and Difobedient, and unto every good Work Reprobate? Shall there be any room left for pretenfe, that the Church hath not Power to do this, which the Apoftles took order with the Churches to have done in both thofe cafes, and which the Church in the firft and pureft times of Chriftianity did accordingly in both cafes?

There is a Paffage in S. *John* 1 Ep. 5. 16. *If any Man fee his Brother Sin a Sin, which is not unto Death, he fhall ask and he fhall give him Life for them that Sin not unto Death: There is a Sin unto Death, I do not fay that he fhall pray for it :* which at firft fight feems to fpeak of Private Prayers of particular Perfons, but yet there is reafon,

to

to think rather it referreth to the Prayers which the Church made on behalf of Penitents, when they were in a way of being restored to the Communion of the Church. For *Tertullian* in many places of his Book *de Pudicitiâ*, argues from this Scripture, that Penance was not to be allowed to Adulterers. The *Novatians* also at the Council of *Nice*, urged it to *Constantine*, as a reason why the Church ought always to refuse Penance to Apostates. And I do not find that it was denied on the part of the Church in either Dispute, that the Place of Scripture referred to Penance, but only that the Church admitted not their consequence. S. *John* was understood by the Church, as well as by them, to speak of, and refer to Penance in that Scripture; but these would have it that S. *John* should therein prescribe to the Church not to grant Penance to Adulterers or Apostates; whereas the Church understood his words, *I do not say that ye shall pray for it*, not to command that such should be admitted to Penance; that is, to allow the Church a Power absolutely to refuse them it, in case it should think so fit; but not to prescribe against the Church's Power of granting it, if that should be thought fit, and most for the intrest of Christianity, and the good of

· such

such Sinners Souls. And as the Church understood the Apostle in this Sense, so indeed his words are hardly Intelligible, unless supposed to refer to the use and practice of Penance in the Church; for how should private Christians judge against what light of Conscience their Neighbour sinneth, to grant or refuse him their Prayers upon it? The Church on the other hand may be well allowed to judge, what Sins the grounds and intrest of Christianity will allow her to admit to Penance, and what the same will oblige her to refuse it to altogether, leaving them to God's judgment.

In the Epistle to the *Hebrews, cap.* 6. 4. when the Apostle saith, *It was not possible that those that fell away should be renewed again to Repentance ;* there is reason to think his meaning to be, that such could not be restored by Penance, as other Sinners were according to the practice of the Church. For as when any are Baptized into Christianity, they may be properly said to be instructed or dedicated to Repentance, because of the Repentance from dead works which they profess; so they that fall into Sins after their Baptism, when they come to submit themselves to the Church for their cure, are no less properly said to be *instructed again,* or *re-*
newed

newed to Repentance, in respect of the Repentance they are directed to go thro' in order to their Reconcilement with God. Now Apostates that *fall away* from Christianity, after evident convictions of its Truth, after their having seen, and after having themselves been partakers of the Power of the Holy Ghost, may not expect the Apostle says to be instructed, or *renewed again to Repentance* by the Church as other Sinners were: And the Apostle's Reason agrees, For *because the Earth that receives Rain, and renders no fruit is nigh unto curfing:* Therefore it is not to be thought that such shall easily obtain God's Grace to resolve them to become sincere Christians, or his Mercy to pardon their wretched Apostasie, and consequently the Church must have reason to refuse to undertake the instructing them again to Repentance, whereof they are not in probability capable, and whereby the Church knows not how to assure their Reconciliation with God, whom they have so highly provoked. And that this is the Apostle's meaning, there is this further ground to conclude; to wit, that it is not reasonable to think that the Apostle should say, It is unpossible that such a one should repent; but this may be, that he should say, *It is impossible that* such a one should

he

be instructed again to Repentance; to wit, by the Church, to let such know that they must not expect that Comfort from the Church; which indeed must be false to its Trust, if the means of Reconciliation were not made by the Church difficult as to such *Sinners*, if so be ever it admitted them to any means at all for their being reconciled. And again, *cap.* 10. 26. the Allusion which the Apostle makes to the custom of the *Jews*, (understood by the *Hebrews* to whom he writes) consisteth in this, that as there was no Sacrifice among them for Apostates, so the Christian Sacrifice of the Prayers of the Church was not to be offered for those that had renounced Christianity. And 'tis also more reasonable to think the Apostle should mean this, than that such should never have benefit from the Sacrifice of Christ, or that there could no hope remain to them of God's Mercy, although they should repent of their wickedness. For supposing them never to be admitted to the means of Reconciliation by the Church; yet after such Persons were remitted wholly to God, there might some hope remain of their finding Mercy with him upon their Repentance; though his Church considering the great wickedness of their Hearts, could not give them af-

I

furance

surance or the hopes thereof. This Interpretation of these Texts, and that before of S. *John*, infer the strictness of Discipline under the Apostles to be such, that some Sins which were of a deep dye, were not admitted to Pennance in order to the Communion of the Church being regained thereby. Howbeit, though difficulty was made of readmitting some sorts of Sins, yet the Church did not understand the Apostle's Order, as Peremptory against their Admission, which was pretended by the *Montanists* and *Novatians*, who therefore were Schismaticks in seperating from the Church, when the whole Church was agreed that there might be an abatement of this strictness, when the Church should see cause and necessity for it. But whether the *Montanists* and *Novatians* were right in their understanding of these Texts, to disallow the Church's Ministerial Power, in the reconciling of such Penitents as had committed heinous Sins, whom they would not have therefore to be received by the Church to Communion again, nor to the Participation of the Holy Mysteries, notwithstanding their Repentance were ever so sound; but to be left wholly to God, and remain separated from his Church, (which was a Thing long disputed in the the *African* Church, and an Opinion held

by

by several that did not think fit to separate from the Church upon it; which was the Crime of the *Montanists* and *Novatians*) or the Church that understood these Scriptures, to imply only a difficulty, as to the re-admitting of such Penitents, that they might not easily find Admission from the Church, though not to take away wholly the Power of the Church, as to the admitting them to her Communion, in case there should be reason to judge their Repentance sincere: It is, however, plain that these Scriptures were understood to refer to a Discipline of the Church, which did instruct Men to Repentance; and did in some cases *renew them again to Repentance*; and even where it might not restore them, there must be implied a Discipline, which put them from that which they might not be restored unto; and if so be that there might nevertheless be a Power for the restoring in all cases though with difficulty; therein will appear the full Ministerial Power of the Church, in the Exclusion of such from Communion with the rest of Christians, as committed heinous Sins inconsistent with their Christian Profession; and in the Reconciliation of such Sinners again by the means of Penance, or a Repentance according to the nature of their Crimes.

I 2   The

of Offenders. To *Timothy* it is given in charge concerning his Perfonal Behaviour in his high Station, that *he be an Example to the Faithful in Word, in Converſation, in Charity, in Fidelity, in Purity,* 1 *Tim.* 4. 12. To *Titus* is given the fame Charge, that *in all things he ſhew himſelf a Pattern of good Works.* Again, as to their uſing all diligence in the Work and Miniſtry to which they were appointed, *Timothy* is charged

1 Tim. 4. 16. *to take heed to himſelf and to his Doctrine, that he might both ſave himſelf and them that*

2 Tim. 4. 2. *heard him,* and to be *inſtant in ſeaſon and*
Tit. 2. 1. 8. *out of ſeaſon. Titus* is alſo charged *to ſpeak the things which become ſound Doctrine,*

cap. 3. 8. therein to ſhew *Uncorruptneſs, Gravity, Sincerity,* and that he affirm conſtantly the neceſſity of *good Works* among Chriſtians. *Timothy* is told how Biſhops and Deacons

1 Tim. 2. ſhould be qualified, that he might know how to behave himſelf in reſpect of them, that is, doubtleſs, both know what manner of Perſons to Admit to thoſe Offices in the Church of God, and ſee the Behaviour of thoſe that were Admitted were anſwerable to their high Character. *Titus*

Tit. 1 5. 6. being left *in Crete to ſet the Church in Order and Ordain* Elders *therein* is alſo put in mind how theſe ſhould be qualified, that the care might lie upon him to Ordain ſuch only, and ſee they continued according to to that Character. Many more things were given in charge to them both alike, but especially in the matter of Discipline, which serveth most our present purpose. *Timothy* is ordered to *charge those* that had part in the Ministry with, and under him, that they *taught no strange Doctrine, nor gave heed to Fables and Genealogies, which ministred Questions rather than godly Edifying.* And that if any *taught otherwise* than according to the *Words* and Truth of our *Lord Jesus* Christ, *and the Doctrine which is according to Godliness*; from such he should *withdraw himself.* *Titus* is also told of *Unruly* and *vain Talkers, and Deceivers, teaching things that they ought not, for filthy Lucres-sake,* and that *the Mouths of such must be stopped,* and that such he should *rebuke sharply, that they might become Sound in the Faith*: and for such of them as were wilful and obstinate in their wicked Errors, that is, *Hereticks, after the first and second Admonition he should reject or avoid.* Where note, that *Timothy*'s being bid to *withdraw himself from such,* and *Titus* to *avoid* or *reject* them, whether you will, are as one and the same thing, amounting to nothing more nor less than a Censure, that might remove such False Teachers from the Church: For in Reason it is to be understood that S. *Paul* prescribes that to

1 Tit. 1. 3. & 4.

1 Tim. 6. 3. & 5.

Tit. 1. 10. 11, & 13.

Timothy and *Titus* which he intends their Flocks should Practife : Suppofing, that being Chriftians, they would be careful to avoid the Infection of thofe whom their Paftors fhould withdraw from and avoid; thereby giving notice that they counted them dangerous, not to themfelves, but to their Flocks. 'Tis alfo to be fuppofed, that Bifhops of a Church in being ordered to withdraw themfelves from, and avoid falfe Teachers, muft underftand it to be their care and duty to fee fuch removed from their Flock, otherwife, how poffibly is it to be thought they fhould withdraw themfelves from fuch ? 'Tis not to be fuppofed they fhould withdraw themfelves from their Flocks, for that fuch have crept in among them ; that were to leave the Flock of Chrift Expofed to their Allurements and Beguilings. Moreover, in reference to the Manners and Lives of Chriftians of all Ranks, which they were concerned fo to infpect and overfee, as to take heed to their being fuch as might *Adorn the Doctrine of God and our Saviour ;* It is required of *Timothy,* that he *command and teach* the things that appertained to Godlinefs, that he *Exhort, Reprove, Rebuke, make full Proof of his Miniftry, let no Man despife his Youth :* As of *Titus* alfo, that he *fpake the things which became found Doctrine,*

m. 4

m. 4
5

ᵗrine, that he *affirm conſtantly that they* Tit. 2. 1.
which have believed in God muſt be careful cap. 3. 8.
to maintain good works, that he exhort and cap. 2. 15
rebuke with all Authority, And, *let no Man
deſpiſe him.* What is to *reprove, rebuke,
make full proof of the Miniſtry,* and to *exhort,
and rebuke with all Authority,* but to make
uſe of all the Authority their Miniſtry
had, to oblige all ſuch as Profeſſed themſelves Chriſtians to be what they Profeſſed.
And how alſo ſhould they keep themſelves
above being *deſpiſed* by any, but if any
Sinners ſhould ſtand it out againſt their
Reproofs and Admonition (as though
*they ſought a Proof of the Power of Chriſt
in them,* or as ſlighting their Charge and
Warning,) by *uſing ſharpneſs according to the
Power which the Lord had given them ?*
Which Extremity of Cenſure, no one that
had any the leaſt fear of God remaining
in him could poſſibly deſpiſe. But S. *Paul*
Writing more largely to *Timothy* than *Titus* about theſe Matters, his Inſtructions to
the former touching his Government of the
Church are more particular and full. Inſomuch that we find particularly (to our
Purpoſe) Rules given for his acting; In *Reproof,* which is the firſt Act of Diſcipline
towards the Amendment of ſuch as may
have done amiſs, that herein he *treat* all
after a becoming, meek, and affectionate
manner,

1 Tim. 5. 1 manner, *an Elder as a Father*, having regard to the Place and Authority that he also has in the Church of God; the *Novices* and meanest Christians as Brethren, kindly and affectionately, therein to make them sensible that his Reproof proceeded not from Imperiousness in his Office, but from the Concern he had for their Souls welfare, and the necessity laid upon him to take Care of the Church of God. In *Rebuke* or *Censure*, that when Offences should make this necessary, he should observe, in order to his having perfect knowledge (always necessary to be had before Judgment pass on any Fault.) In the Case of an *Elder, not to receive an Accusation* against *him, unless from two or three Witnesses*, (the Reason to be presumed this, that it being their Office to Reprove the Faults of others, for that cause, they likely are hated by such, whose Deeds they Reprove, and upon that very often falsely accused). Which Caution to a Bishop of the Church must be understood by him to imply it his Concern in every one's Case to be rightly informed. And after this he may spare no kind or sort of Offenders or Offences; *Them that Sin, Re-* 1 Tim. 5. 20. *buke before all, that others also may fear. I charge thee before God and the Lord Jesus Christ and the Elect Angels, that thou observe*

these

these things without preferring one before another, doing nothing by partiality. So strict a Charge as this plainly importeth a necessity on him to fulfil the Trust of his Ministry in this Instance especially, as also that the matter is of great moment and consequence to the Church of God. He must then you see, *Rebuke them that Sin, before all, i. e.* Such as shall have committed any Scandalous Offence (whom for not Reforming after Admonition, it shall be necessary to Rebuke more *sharply* and to Censure), he must Rebuke openly before all, that is, in the presence of the Community of Christians. Wherein I mark the Intrest of the Congregation in this work of Discipline, as Censures of this kind were to Pass in their Publick Assemblies, (at which, as the People bewailed the case of the Sinner, and prayed on his behalf that the Censure might work the Cure of his Sin, so the Church received satisfaction for the Scandal, by the removal of the Person that had given it, from the Privileges which the Faithful enjoyed, and none others had right to enjoy): And the two great causes that good, and well-meaning Christians may have to take Offence at those that have the Ministry of Discipline in the Church, if Sinners, guilty of Notorious Crimes, of whose amend-

amendment there is no appearance go unrebuked, and without Cenfure, be fuffered to continue in the Church, and have fhare in its Communion. But this Cenfure of Offenders was to be thus Publick, *that others might fear,* be kept from falling into the like fins, by fear of coming under the fame Cenfure themfelves, and not only this, but that they might have fear alfo concerning the State and Condition of their Souls, in reference to Sins not known, and conclude that if Vicious Perfons, whofe Sins are known cannot be Tolerated within the Church, but muft be Excluded from it, as not having Right or Share in the Promifes of God; even they themfelves being guilty of Sins committed in fecret, have reafon to fear, as to the Cafe of their Souls; left being guilty before God of Sins inconfiftent with Chriftianity, their Intereft in God's Mercy as to the forgivenefs of their fins fhould be likewife forfeited. But let notice be alfo taken, that S. *Paul* does here conjure *Timothy* by all that is Sacred and Holy as to do his Duty herein, fo to Act uprightly in it; When he *chargeth him before God and the Lord Jefus Chrift, and the Elect, or Holy Angels,* is it not a Charge as himfelf muft expect to anfwer before God and the Lord Jefus Chrift, when the *Son of Man fhall come*

in

in his Glory, and all the Holy Angels with him, for the fulfilling of his Miniftry in this particular, that he *obferve* to do his Duty therein? And that he Execute this Difcipline χωεὶς πεοχειματ⌀., *without prejudice,* which in a judicial fenfe fignifies *Præcipitancy* in Condemning a Perfon, not allowing, or not regarding the Defence he may make for himfelf; or *Præ-judging* upon Refpect, where he that fhould Judge the Matter, is præpoffeffed with an ill Opinion of the Party ftanding to be Judged, or, that *Prejudice,* which 'tis poffible for a Judge to have againft a Man out of particular Hatred or Ill-will. Nothing of this fhould have the leaft place, fo much as in the Mind of him that is entrufted with this Difcipline, or acteth in any part of its Miniftry; much lefs fhould it be fuffered to influence any thing done thereupon. Farther it is given him in charge, that herein he *do nothing by Partiality* κατὰ πρόσκλιον, out of *inclination,* in favour to any Man's Caufe, or any Man's Perfon. The Apoftle feems in both Expreffions to refer to the Command in the Law, *Exod.* 23: 1, 2. *Not to Judge on falfe Report,* and again, *not to decline after any to wreft Judgment.* We fhall not wonder at the ftrictnefs of the Apoftle's Charge about the execution of this Difcipline, and the laying

ing aside all Prejudice and Partiality therein; if we confider the Difcipline as a Part
of the Gofpel-Miniftry, and the Procefs
of fuch Cenfure and the Judgment thereof as Paffing in the Church of God. The
Truft alfo concerning it, as given and
committed by him *with whom there is no
refpect of Perfons*: And that there muft be
a peculiar Concern on thofe that Cenfure
other Mens Sins, that themfelves do not
fin in the doing it, (as they will, if either
they forget the Chriftian Spirit and Temper of meeknefs and Charity, or have
not a true regard to do what is Juft, and
to do it impartially, or not a regard to
the End of God and our Saviour, in the
Inftitution of this Difcipline, which is the
Reformation of the Sinner, and bringing
him to Repentance): And that even the
Importance of the thing requires the ftricteft Charge, and the greateft Care; the
Souls of Men and their Salvation; the Honour of Religion and Propagation of the
fame; the Unity of Chrift's Church, and
the Edification thereof in Righteoufnefs,
being all concerned, and in a great meafure, depending on the due, and rightly
faithful and impartial exercife of this Difcipline in God's Church. But to look
farther into *Timothy's* Inftructions about
this matter; S. *Paul* having thus required
and

and Charged him to do his Duty, and proceed against *them that Sin,* and should not repent them of their wickedness, by *Rebuke* and *Censure,* goes on to instruct him how to act after this, so as his Censure might have its Effect, according to the End of God and our Saviour, in the Power and Authority given him, for the Reformation and Amendment of such Sinners. This I take to be the meaning of his next words, *Lay hands suddenly on no Man, neither be partaker of other Men's Sins,* that is to say, As he had Power of Judging, whom to Admit, and whom not to Admit to Penance after such Censure, and might not of right admit to it any but such as he should have reason to think, *being pricked in their heart* out of concern for their guilt and danger, were sincerely desirous of being Admitted to the Prayers of God's Church, and to be instructed by its Ministry in the Way and Work of Repentance: So he should take heed to act conscientiously, and wisely, and warily in this particular also of his Trust, not easily admitting to Penance such Offenders (this being the means, which consequently must give hope of their Reconciliation with the Church) and especially not suddenly receiving any such to the *Peace* and *Communion* of the Church again.

again. And the reason he adds by way of suggestion is such as must have obliged him to take special care in this matter, *left he be partaker of other Men's Sins,* that is, those sins which his Censure (according to the intent of God and Christ, upon whose Authority he acted therein) should have reformed in such Offenders, but would not do so, if he granted Penance to them that were not fit for it, and especially if before they had approved their Repentance and Reformation, they were received to the Communion of the Church again.

This I take to be the Apostle's Sense, for that *Imposition of hands,* was a Ceremony in use in the Church, during the Prescript time of Penance ; and also when Penitents were received into the Communion of the Church. The Custom was, that those of that state, after the earnest Prayers of the Congregation to God on their behalf, came and kneeled before the Bishop ; who holding his Hands over their Heads, with his Blessing and Prayers to God for their Pardon, dismissed them before the Mysteries : This was called on their part ὑπόπτωσις, or falling down, on his part χειροθεσία, or Imposition of Hands in Penance : The like Imposition of Hands was, when they *conferred the Indulgence of*
Recon-

Reconciliation ; which was the admitting them to the Penance of the Church, and to full Communion with the Faithful. To this purpoſe, antiently ſome Offenders re-moved from the Church, could *not have hands laid on them as Penitents* ; could not be admitted to Penance, at leaſt not till after ſome time: And others might not be *reconciled*, or reſtored to the Com-munion of the Church, till the Courſe of their Penance was gone thorough, which in ſome caſes was a long ſpace of time. I know this Text of the Apoſtle is gene-rally underſtood in another Senſe, as re-ferring to *Ordination of Miniſters* ; yet, for the ſame reaſon which he alledgeth, it may be extended to all Acts of the Church that are bleſſed by the Prayers thereof, with Impoſition of hands. For if *Timothy* by impoſing hands upon thoſe whom he *ordains*, become acceſſary to their Sins, if they be unfit to be *ordained*; by the ſame reaſon, if he impoſe hands ; that is, grant Penance to, or reſtore to the Communion of the Church, ſuch as are not fit for it, he becomes acceſſary to the Sins, which they would probably have repented of and amended, had the Diſcipline of the Church been ſtrict over them ; but which through his Remiſneſs they may have nei-ther repented, nor forſaken. But I need

K   not

not argue from Parity of Reason, that the Apostle may be understood in this Sense, when the Context and Coherence of his Discourse oblige, that he be thus understood; for *ver.* 20. as you have seen, there is direction for the *Publick rebuking* of Offenders and censuring them; and *ver.* 21. a most solemn and strict charge to the same purpose, as also against *prejudging* on one side, and *partiality* or favour on the other. Whatever different Sense therefore, his words *Lay hands suddenly on no Man*, &c. may bear, if they may be interpreted in a Sense agreeable to the business in hand, which was *Church Censure,* they shall most properly be understood in it. Such is this, that *Timothy* should use *deliberation* and *delay*, in order to observe the Penitent's disposition and behaviour, before he admit him to Penance after Censure, and should by no means restore him to the Communion of the Church, before the sincerity of his Repentance and Reformation be approved to him; according as in the Primitive Practice and Canons, some Offenders were refused Penance, and most that were admitted to it, must exercise themselves for some space in good Works, before they were thought fit to be restored. In all which the Aim was that the Censure of Discipline might be
effectual

effectual to its end, the Reformation of the Sinner and the saving his Soul; which was likely to come to pass, if Offenders under Censure were forced to seek *their place of Repentance,* i. e. room and place for themselves among Penitents in the Church, by such Humility and Sorrow as might be a Mortification of their Pride of Heart, and dispose them to *Sorrow unto Repentance;* and if also they could not be restored to the Communion of the Church, till the Course of their Repentance were seen performed in such a manner, as might give ground to think them with true Sorrow, and Contrition of Heart to have sought Reconcilement with God, and to be in the right way of obtaining it: But on the other hand very unlikely to come to pass, if the Discipline should not be strict, for the humbling of those that came to seek the Ministry of Reconciliation, and for constraining them to go through the course of Humiliation and Repentance, which that Ministry ought to prescribe, in order to their Reconciliation with God, and ought also to see performed, before it assure their hopes concerning such Reconciliation.

Now these Scriptures which we have thus inspected, affording us so many Instances of Acts done by the Apostles and

the Difciples of our Lord, in purfuance
of the Power given by him to his Church
under the Figure of the *Keys of his Houfe*,
as alfo divers plain References to fome
Courfe and Order taken by the Apoftles
with the Churches of their Planting, for
this Power to be exercifed therein, for the
Government of the fame by a due Difcipline, and likewife fome direct and po-
fitive Orders of this nature, exprefly charging that the power of the Miniftry be employed to this purpofe; we muft be paft
doubt, that the Apoftles in their time, un-
derftanding their Power in Chrift, took
order with the Churches and delegated a
Power to the Miniftry thereof for Government and Difcipline.

C H A P. IV.

THE Reafons hitherto advanced,
therefore having as I think, made
fufficient Proof, that the *Power of the Keys*
was Exercifed by the Apoftles in the Government of the Church, and that they
gave order for a Difcipline in the Churches
of their Planting, for the felf-fame purpofe, with Power accordingly; I hold it
conve-

convenient that the practice of Diſcipline according to them and the Churches in their time, which may be Collected in parts from the Scriptures that refer to, and point them out to us, be here placed together, and fitted for our view at once.

Now the Power of the Keys and Diſcipline that employeth it are viſible : Firſt, in *Baptiſm,* or the Admiſſion of Diſciples into the Church of Chriſt by that Ceremony. I mean, not in the Baptizing or Act of Admiſſion it ſelf, but in the way of Admiſſion and Grant of that Sacrament, that is to ſay, in the preparing Men for, and in procuring in them the diſpoſition that made them fit for that Admiſſion, fit to have Baptiſm conferred on them; and in acting according to a Truſt that muſt be ſuppoſed in the Power that was to do this, ſo as to judge in whom that Diſpoſition was wrought, and who were fit Perſons to be Admitted into the Church of Chriſt by this means. This is a Thing that hath not been yet under our conſideration, becauſe the Diſcipline which my deſign engaged me immediately to conſider, is that which ſuppoſeth Men to be Chriſtians, and is concerned to keep them ſuch; nevertheleſs it is fit we take notice that there was a Diſcipline to inſtruct and prepare ſuch as offered themſelves to the Church

K 3

for

for Baptifm concerning the Profeffion they were to make therein, and their refolution to fulfil what they took upon them: and that this Difcipline likewife had its beginning from the Apoftles, and was grounded alfo on the *Power of the Keys.* For this appearing, there will appear with it the Reafon and Ground of This, that is, the Subject of my prefent Argument. For, fuppofe a Power fetled in the Church by God to judge who is fit to be Admitted into it, and a Difcipline to prepare for that Admiffion, and the fame Power enabled to Refufe fuch as fhall be judged unfit; by the fame reafon fhall there be a Difcipline to Govern thofe that are within the Church, and keep them to their Profeffion, and Power to Exclude fuch as prove themfelves unfit to be of the Church after they are Admitted to it. Be it obferved then, that from the beginning there was a Power in the Church of judging whether Men were fit for its Baptifm or not, as alfo a Difcipline to bring them to be fit for it; and this Power of Baptizing was a different thing from the Office of Miniftring it: The Truft of this Power indeed was generally lodged in the fame hands that Miniftred the Office, yet fo as that Truft obliged them, not to confer Baptifm but on fuch as were qualified

ed

ed for it. This is what we in the present state of the Church do not distinguish,
because all are born within the Pale of the
Church, and by Order thereof Baptized
Infants; But which we may see ground
to distinguish, if we rightly consider the
Words of our Lord, charging his Apostles
to *make Disciples of all Nations, Baptizing
them in the Name of the Father, Son, and
Holy Ghost*, therein requiring them, first
to bring Men to be Disciples, and then to
Baptize them: that is, first to bring Men
to submit to the Gospel, and to a Resolution of *doing God's Will*, according to our
Lord's saying, that those that will *do his
Father's Will are his Disciples*, and then to
Admit them into the Church by Baptism.
Which supposeth a judgment whether such
submitted to the Gospel or not, and a Trust
in those that Ministred Baptism, to judge
of the same, and bring to pass what might
be wanting, before they granted any Admission into the Church by that means. I
take it to be from a sense of this Trust
lodged within the Church as to Baptism,
that our Church of *England* requireth a
Contract and Stipulation on behalf of those
whom it Baptizeth in their Infancy, and
that it also giveth it in charge to all that
have the Cure of Souls, to Instruct and
Catechise all that were thus Baptized,

K 4 and

and prepare and fit them for *Confirmation,*
at which it requires all such *openly before
the Church to Ratify and Confirm their
Baptismal Engagement, and Promise that
they will ever more endeavour themselves
faithfully to observe the same.* But whether
we take this to proceed from the sense of
such a Trust or not, it plainly appeareth
that there was such a Trust and Power
lodged with the Church, and Proceedings
accordingly in the time of the Apostles.
For what S. *Peter* speaks of the *Answer of
a good Conscience to God* in Baptism, 1 *Pet.*
3. 21. Sheweth, that in time of the Apostles, (which must therefore be upon their
Order), Interrogatories were propounded
to them that were to be Baptized, in the
nature of a Contract between the Church
and them, wherein they obliged themselves to live according to the Gospel as
Disciples, and thereupon had Admission
into the Church.   This must be the Effect
of a Trust in the Church to see those that
were Baptized, first brought to a Resolution of living as Christians. S. *Peter* himself seems to have acted upon this Trust
and Power, in giving order for the Baptizing of *Cornelius and his Friends.* Its true,
there was a Prejudice in him and those of
the Circumcision against them as *Gentiles,*
which might make him backward to Baptize

Acts 10
47.

tize fuch into the Church of Chrift, tho'
he had no Power to have refufed Baptifm
to any; but if we obferve, that Prejudice
feems to have been removed by the Vifion,
upon which he refolved to go with the
Meffengers that *Cornelius* had fent for him;
and not only fo, but to *Cornelius* and thofe
that were with him, *to hear all things that
were Commanded him of God*; he makes no
fcruple to fay, *of a Truth I perceive that
God is no Refpecter of.Perfons, but in every
Nation he that feareth him and worketh Righteoufnefs is accepted with him,* and thereupon he Preacheth to them Chrift Crucifi'd
and giveth them hope out of the Prophets,
that *whofoeverBelieveth in him fhould receive
Remiffion of Sins.* When he reafoneth therefore after this, faying, *Can any Man forbid
Water that thefe fhould not be Baptized, which
have received the Holy Ghoft as well as we ?*
And thereupon *commanded them to be Baptized in the Name of the Lord Jefus;* Seemeth it not to be upon this Prefumption,
that they having vifibly received the Holy
Ghoft after that manner upon his Preaching, would not be deftitute of the Grace of
the fame Holy Spirit, to refolve and enable them, to live as God's People, and
therefore might, and ought to be Received
by Baptifm into the Church of Chrift?
Which feemeth alfo yet more plainly to
appe.r

appear from what he argueth in defence
of that which he had done in this matter
to the Brethren at *Jerusalem* , when ,
relating his own Vision, and what *Cornelius* had told him of his having seen an
Angel that bid him send for *Peter*, who
should tell him words whereby he and his
House should be saved, as also what came
to pass as he was Preaching these Words
to them, that the *Holy Ghost fell on them,*
which brought to his remembrance the
saying of the Lord, how that his followers should be *Baptized with the Holy Ghost;*
he addeth thereupon, *Forasmuch then as*
God gave them the like Gift as he did unto
us *who believed on the Lord Jesus, what*
was I, that I could withstand God? that is
to say, how could he refuse them Baptism,
it appearing that God had given them the
like Grace, as they who had so believed
on the Lord Jesus, as to give themselves
to be Gods' People, walking after his
Will now according to Christ Jesus? And
to this purpose it seemeth that he was understood by those of the Circumcision,
who being silenced, and resting satisfied
with what he had done, are said to have
Glorified God, saying, Then hath God also
to the *Gentiles* granted *Repentance* unto
Life : concluding hence, that there was
ground to think that they also would
through

Acts ,11.
17.

through Grace *repent* of their wicked living, and come to live as the People of God, and thereby with them, attain to Life Eternal. This maketh it a plain Case to me, that S. *Peter*, though at first, prejudiced as a *Jew*, against the *Gentiles*, did not however dispute the Baptism of *Cornelius* and *his Friends* altogether upon account of that Prejudice, but as one entrusted with the Baptism of Christ, judged rightly that they might, and accordingly, commanded them to be Baptized, having ground sufficient to presume that they would live as Christians who had received the *Holy Ghost* in so visible a manner, that *gift* supposing the gift of Grace also from God for this purpose. But again, what the Apostle speaks, *Heb.* 6. 2. of the *foundation of Repentance from dead Works, the Doctrine of Baptism and Imposition of Hands*, manifestly refers to that which was a Custom in the Church, that they which offered themselves to Baptism, should be instructed in the Doctrine of the Gospel, and prepared to enter into contract with the Church on God's behalf, to forsake such courses of the World as were inconsistent with the Profession of Holiness they were now to make. How is the *foundation* of Christianity *laid in Repentance from Dead Works*, but in shewing

the

the necessity of this to prepare Men to become Christians? The *Doctrine of Baptism* also, doubtless signifying, that Doctrine or Summ of Christian Truth, which the *Catechumens* were taught before Baptism; called also the Doctrine of Imposition of Hands, because the use was, that they who came to be instructed by the *Catechist* were dimissed from him with Imposition of Hands and a Prayer, that they might in due time become good Christians. All visible marks of the Power of the Church in judging whether Men were fit for Baptism or not, and of a Discipline therein to fit them for it. If to this it be objected, that we read in Scripture of great numbers, *Three Thousand in a day added to the Church,* who could not be supposed to be thus Instructed and judged of; my Answer is, that what was done in cases where the extraordinary hand of God appeared in Men's Conversion, and at the beginning, before a Church was gathered to Christ, till after which there could not be Order; is not to be made an Objection against what there is manifest reason to suppose done afterwards when the Church came to be setled in a regular method, and course taken for the due execution of its Ministry according to Rule. The things afore said therefore being rightly consider'd,

I do

I do not think it will be denied me, that the Church had a Trust committed with the Power of granting Baptism, and that this Power being a Branch of that Power given by Christ, under the Figure of the Keys of his House, appeared, as did also its Discipline, in the Preparatory Instructions that were always used therein, to fit Men for its Baptism; and in the not granting this till after such Preparation, and granting it when there was reason to judge that they who sought it, were brought to such a disposition as had resolved them to undertake Christianity with a good Conscience; *i. e.* to be sincere in that undertaking.

And certainly if the Church found it self concerned by Discipline to prepare Men for its Baptism, and had Power to refuse the admitting such into the Church of Christ, whom it sees no Reason to hope well of, as to their sincerity in undertaking, or stedfastness in abiding by, what they must undertake as Christians; then it hath been concluded aright and well, that the Church is concerned by a Discipline to keep Men to the performance of what they took upon them, when they first made Profession of Christianity, and were admitted into the Church of Christ; and then also is the Power of excluding those,

those, who undertake this and perform it not, well grounded. Accordingly we find the Power and Discipline of the Church from the beginning, employed to this purpose ; namely, in taking care of, and seeing to such as were esteemed worthy, as being qualified by professing a Resolution to do the Will of God, to be baptized into his Church, and were admitted accordingly, that they discharged that Profession and Resolution in their Lives. This was the *Government* of the Church in Godliness, frequently spoken of in Scripture, and given in charge to them whom the *Holy Ghost* had made *Overseers* in God's Church, when they were required to *take heed* to themselves and to their Flock, to *rule with diligence,* and to *rule well* the Church of God, to *watch* and *labour* in doing the *work* of their Ministry, as considering the end of the same towards the Children of God. But if any notwithstanding, *professing* that they *knew God, in their works denied him,* and were *disobedient,* then was there cause for the Church to *make proof of its Ministry,* as it did with Authority, *admonishing, reproving, rebuking* such Sinners ; yet this *in meekness* hitherto, trying to *restore* them if possible, and waiting *if God peradventure would give them Repentance to the acknowledging of the Truth,*

and

and that they might recover themselves out of the Snare of the Devil. To this purpose was it given in charge, That if a *Man were overtaken in a fault,* the Spiritual *should restore such an one in the Spirit of meekness.* Also to such as were entrusted with the Ministry, *to warn,* to *admonish, to charge,* to *exhort, reprove, rebuke* as with *authority,* so with *all long-suffering.* But when these means could not work their Effect, so as to prevail with them that had sinned, to repent them of their wickedness; or when their wickedness was so foul as to be a Shame and Reproach to the Christian Religion, to leave no hope for God's favour to such Presumptuous Sinners; nor hope to the Church, as to the amendment of such, having profligate and *seared Consciences*; then did the Church make use of its Power in Christ, to cut off and exclude such Sinners from the Church of Christ; Thereby to make them sensible, that they were cut off from all hope and interest in God's Promises, relating to the forgiveness of Sins and Eternal Life; their Intrest in these being lost by their Relapse into Sins; which forsaking before in hope of God's Promises for these things the Church had allowed, and made them Partakers of according to its Power in Christ; but now by the same

Power

Power excluded them from difannulling all their Hopes or pretended Intreft in God's Favour, or Mercy as forfeited and loft. This appeareth by what S. *Paul* did in the cafe of the *Inceftuous* Perfon at *Corinth,* and *others* whom he *delivered to Satan*; by the blame he layeth on that Church, for neglect of duty in that they *had not put away him that had done that Evil deed from among them*; by his prefling them at length to do their duty in the cafe, in the executing of his Sentence, (which though it might have more in it, than barely the cutting off that Perfon from the Communion of the Church; yet whatfoever there might be more, was certainly at that time only the confequent of that Cenfure); by his threatning others *that had finned, and fhould not have repented them of their wickednefs,* that he would not *fpare them,* when he fhould come to *Corinth*; that he would *ufe fharpnefs according to the Power which the Lord had given him:* by the charge given to thofe who were beft in Truft with the Miniftry, as particularly to *Timothy* and *Titus,* to *rebuke with all authority,* and to let *none defpife them, to make full proof of their Miniftry,* to rebuke them that Sin *before all, that others might fear,* and to act herein *without prejudice,* and *without partiality*; (with more of this nature, which 'tis

'tis needlefs to repeat here, having been already confidered at large). But now even after this Cenfure, the Church ftill continued to have care as concerning the Effects of its Difcipline, that it might be a means to bring fuch Sinners to *Sorrow* unto Repentance, that the *Spirit might be faved in the day of the Lord :* It waited therefore for, and watched what effect its Cenfure had on fuch Sinners, and in cafe they became fenfible upon it of their Sin and Danger, and fought Peace with the Church, and Reconcilement with God, by the means of its Miniftry ; then did the Church take upon it felf the care of *inftructing them to Repentance*; and upon the Penitent's fubmitting to, and going thorough with that Courfe of Repentance, which upon the beft judgment that could be made of the State, and Circumftances of the Sinner, and nature of the Offence was thought neceffary ; there was an abatement or Relaxation of the Cenfure, the Penitent's Sorrow and Repentance appearing. This is feen in what S. *Paul* did at *Corinth,* upon the Submiffion and Sorrow of the *Inceftuous* Perfon, whom he had before put under Cenfure, whom as I faid before, the Apoftle feems to have admitted to Penance, in order to his being reftored, or (as more commonly that act

L   of

of his is underſtood) to have granted full Reconcilement with the Church, as thinking and judging him to have *ſorrowed after a godly ſort,* and ſo by his True Repentance to be in the way of obtaining Reconciliation with God alſo. Only in caſe the Sin were very great, ſuch as neceſſarily implied the Offender to be of a profligate Conſcience, and unlikely to become a True Penitent; or the guilt ſuch as it could not be ſuppoſed the Divine Mercy would eaſily forgive, or as the Church could not readily admit to the hope of forgiveneſs, but it muſt be liable to ſcandal in its Miniſtry, as giving countenance to Sin; the Church then found it ſelf under a neceſſity to uſe great deliberation in the admitting ſuch Offenders to Penance, and to preſcribe a long courſe of Penance, and ſee it gone through in ſuch a manner, as might give ſome Preſumption of the Penitent's ſincerity, and of a change in the Hearts of ſuch, before the Cenſure were taken off; and in ſome caſes it was not thought fit at all to admit the Offenders ſo much as to Penance, to any hope or means of Reconciliation with the Church; but to leave them altogether to the Mercy of God, and to the bewailing of their Sins, if peradventure God might give them Repentance and ſhew them

them Mercy. Therefore as I said was it given in charge to *Timothy*, that he should *Lay hands suddenly on no Man, neither be partaker of other Mens Sins* ; spoken doubtless in reference to Imposition of hands in Penance, (a way of Benediction used in reconciling Sinners to the Church) to intimate to him, that if this were hastily done without care to procure in such true Repentance, and without knowledge of its being wrought in them, upon himself would lie much of the guilt of such Sins, as those Sinners thinking themselves in the way of Salvation, by being admitted to the Station of Penitents, or restored to the Communion of the Church thus easily, might continue to live in, and on him also would be chargeable the mischiefs which such disorder and scandal must occasion in the Church, to the prejudice of true Religion and Godliness. And to this purpose also is that of the Apostle, in his Epistle to the *Hebrews,* where he saith, *It was impossible,* that those who *fell away* after having been *once* enlightned, and *having tasted of the Heavenly gift, and been partakers of the Holy Ghost,* &c. which must suppose their Sin Presumptuous, and done in *despite of God's grace,* should be *renewed again to Repentance* ; to wit, by the Church ; to let such Sinners know

L 2   that

that they muſt not expect the Church *to*
give them any aſſurance of their Reconciliation with God after ſuch Sins. As
that of S. *John* concerning the *Sin unto
Death, not to be prayed for,* intimateth that
the Church might not take upon it to do
in this as in other caſes; *i. e.* to intercede
with God by Prayers on their behalf, as
for other Sinners ; Sins of ſo great a guilt
being utterly inconſiſtent with the hope of
Salvation, which hope therefore it became
not the Church to give unto ſuch Sinners ;
but leave them to expect what God might
do of his Infinite and Extraordinary Mercy, and deny them the hope uſually given
to other Penitents, to make ſuch wretched
Sinners the more ſolicitous and humble in
bewailing their Sins, and to deter others
the more, that they might not dare or
preſume to do wickedly in ſuch manner.
This was the Practice and Method of
Diſcipline, according to the Apoſtles and
in the Churches of their time; which the
ſeveral Parts thereof referred to in ſeveral
Scriptures occaſionally, being put together
make out.

CHAP.

CHAP. V.

LET us but compare now the Practice of the Primitive Church, with this that we find done in time of the Apostles, and as the Correspondence will be clear, so that Correspondence will clear up to us the Practice pointed and referred to in the Scriptures, (that have been considered by us) to be such, as we have conceived it from the hints and intimations given us therein.

Now the Primitive Discipline was this. The Church as looking on it self under a Trust by having the Power of Baptism, did therefore concern it self to engage all those, who embraced Christianity, to a Profession thereof, and a Resolution to live after it; and upon these terms only would the Church admit Men by its Baptism into the House of God. For this purpose, as it demanded of those who were baptized, that they solemnly renounced the Vices of the Age, and the wicked courses of the World; so did it take care on behalf of them that had been won to believe the Truth of Christianity, that they should be instructed as in Chri-

L 3   stian

ſtian Truth; ſo in the neceſſity of making
a Profeſſion of Chriſtian Life, and of en-
gaging in that Profeſſion with ſincerity.
There is nothing more evident in the
practice of the whole Church from the beginning than this, That there was a Time
allowed and required by the Church for
thoſe that profeſſed themſelves converted,
to believe the Truth of Chriſtianity, to
give Trial of their Converſation, that it
might be ſeen whether in likelihood they
would apply themſelves to live like Chriſtians, and what aſſurance or preſumption
the Church might conceive that they would
not betray the Profeſſion thereof, before
they were admitted to Baptiſm. During
this time of Trial theſe Scholars and
Learners of Chriſtianity, were Catechiſed
and inſtructed not only what to believe,
but how to behave themſelves as Chriſtians,
admitted to converſe among Chriſtians, to
come to their Aſſemblies, and to be preſent
and bear part in ſome of the things of
God's Service; as in the Praiſes of God,
and hearing the Scriptures Read and Expounded, and were diſmiſſed with the
Church's Prayers; that by God's Grace
they might be reſolved to make a good Profeſſion and to be good Chriſtians. This
appears in *Clemens Alexandrinus* his *Pæda-*
gogus, in the *Apoſtolical Conſtitutions*, and
in

in many other Writers of Church Matters; but especially in the distinct Offices of the Church, called *Missa Catechumenorum,* and *Missa Fidelium,* the former, That part of the Office of the Church, which the *Catechumens,* the *Scholars,* or *Probationers* in Christianity were admitted to, the latter, That which was Peculiar to Believers; that is, those that were *Baptized Christians.* There was some difference as to the time for these to be instructed upon what terms they might expect to be saved by Christ, and for Trial of their Conversation, in reference to the Profession they were to make, when they came to be Baptized; some Churches appointing it longer, others shorter; but in all Churches a Time was appointed, and means Preparatory for this purpose, and Baptism not granted otherwise, unless a Man's Zeal to Christianity were found extraordinary, so that there could be no Reason to suspect or doubt his sincerity; for then the Regular time of continuing in the State and Rank of a *Catechumen,* or Scholar in Christianity was frequently abridged by the Church; there being cause for such to be received without farther Trial. Moreover, there were Constitutions and Orders which required Extraordinary Trial of some Persons, as particularly of those

that

that had practised any sort of Magick, that it might be certain they had parted with such Superstitions altogether, before they should be admitted into the number of Christians; and likewise that Men of some particular Professions, and Trades of Life, should not be admitted to Baptism, unless they would profess to leave them, as inconsistent with Christianity: For instance, such as lived by the *Stews,* by the *Stage,* by Soothsaying and Fortune-telling, &c. For in as much as no Man could be Baptized, but he must undertake to live like a Christian, these therefore could not be admitted into the Church, without promise to leave those ways of Life in the World, which the Church must reasonably think, would if they were not left, engage them in wicked Practices. This Practice shews the Primitive Church to have looked on it self to have a Power to judge who were fit to be admitted to its Baptism, and not only so, but to have a Trust that none might be admitted, but such as were duly qualified by a Resolution of renouncing all wicked ways, and the undertaking of God's Service, to be admitted to the hope of his Favour and Grace: Forasmuch as the Acts of the Church in this case were the same, as we must suppose them to have been, had never

ver so plain a charge been given concerning this Trust and Power.

Now this Power and Trust of Admitting into the Church by Baptism, and bringing Men to make a Profession of Christianity at their Admission into the Church of Christ, supposing by consequence of right Reason, the like Power and Trust as to all those who Professed themselves Christians, to keep them to their Profession; and as to those who should fall into sins destructive of Christianity, and contrary to their first Covenant with God and his Church, to put these into danger of being excluded again from the House of God, and even actually to exclude them, if there should not be hope of their amendment, and not to restore them to the Advantages and Privileges of God's Church, until they should give better satisfaction of their Sincerity in Christianity: For this purpose we find a Discipline in the Primitive Church, (grounded as upon the Practice and Order of the Apostles, so upon knowledge of its own Power in Christ, who gave to his Church the Keys of his House) and Exhortations, Admonitions, Reproofs, and Censures, employed in respect of those that had visibly transgressed their Christian Profession, to bring them to acknowledge
their

their Offences, and conftrain them to take courfe for their Repentanc and Amendment.   This is to be feen in *Tertullian's* Words, *Apolog. Cap.* 39. Speaking thus of their Affemblies. *Ibidem etiam Exhortationes, Caftigationes & Cenfura Divina: nam & judicatur magno cum pondere ut apud certos de Dei confpectu,* &c. *There alfo are Exhortations, Reproofs, and the Cenfure of God; for judgment is given with great weight, as among Men affured of God's fight.* He could not have faid this, had it not been known and cuftomary for fuch Exhortations, Reproofs, and Cenfures to be at their Affemblies, for Remedy of the Faults of fuch among them, who lived not as Chriftians, and for their Amendment for the future. He fpeaks in the fame place of a Man's Offending fo *ut à Communicatione Orationis & Conventûs, & omnis Sancti commercii relegetur,* fo as to be *confined from the Communion of Prayers and Affemblies, and all holy Commerce.* Which is a plain Proof that the Church in his time accounted it felf to have Power thus to Cenfure Refractory Sinners, and did fo Cenfure them. Which alfo appears more plainly in the Conteft which *Montanus* and *Tertullian* himfelf (who followed *Montanus* herein) had with the Church, that the Crimes of Apoftacy and Adultery fhould not be admitted to Penance

nance, or to any hopes of Reconcilement
with God by means of the Church. This
Dispute muft neceffarily fuppofe a Difcipline in the Church that put away thefe
and other Sinners from the Church, until
they fhould Repent them of their Wickednefs, as alfo, that Penance was the way
and means by which fuch finners as were
put out of the Church might be reftored
to its Communion again, and that this
way was appointed of neceffity, becaufe
the Church could not re-admit fuch Sinners to its Communion, until there were
ground to think that by Repentance they
had recovered God's Favour, forfeited by
their Sins. Thefe things, I fay, are plainly
fuppofed in the Difpute, let it be, that thefe
great Crimes, about which the Difpute
was, might, or might not be Reconciled
by Penance: and even as to thefe, the
Difpute fuppofeth a Difcipline in the
Church that cut them off from its Communion, to which it would not allow
them by Penance to be Reftored: And had
there not been a Difcipline to this purpofe,
they might with much more reafon have
contended with the Church for fuffering
fuch to abide within it, than for reftoring
them by means of Penance. The Church
neverthelefs having difcharged its Duty,
in removing from it all fuch as were guilty
of

of such Sins, would not suffer the Austerity which *Montanus* and his Followers Affected, to be Imposed upon it for a Rule; For though it was understood, there was cause to fear that the Church, in warranting Pardon to those who might not prove qualified for it, might become chargeable with their Sins, according to S. *Paul, Lay hands suddenly on no Man, nor partake in other Men's Sins*; and that S. *John,* and the Apostle to the *Hebrews* seemed to direct the Church to make difficulty of re-admitting such Sinners; yet it was concluded, that upon the Example of S. *Paul,* who had re-admitted the Incestuous Person at *Corinth,* as reasonably satisfied of the Truth of his Repentance, the Church likewise might re-admit them to its Communion, or to Penance, the means of Réconcilement, when they made suit for it, and should have gone through such a course of Humiliation as might shew them truly Penitent. But yet, still the Church, that it might be able better to answer its Trust to God, in not warranting the Pardon of Sin without reasonable Tryal of Repentance, took a course of lengthning the time of Penance, during which, the Conversation of the Penitent might yield assurance of it, and this according to the Nature of Men's Sins, not allowing some

Recon-

Reconcilement with the Church till the point of Death: The Reason which *Montanus* and his Followers urged, That great Sins might not be admitted to Reconcilement with the Church, That such Sinners might not think it a small matter to Offend in such manner, nor that God's Pardon might be soon obtained, prevailing with the Church not to suffer such Sinners to be lightly admitted, that from the difficulty of their Penance and Admission, they might be convinced of difficulty in Repenting of such Sins, and difficulty of re-gaining God's Favour, or the hope of his Favour after them: and that those, and all others might in that respect fear to Offend. After those times, when the Customs of the Church in force, before they came in Writing, came to be reduced into Writing for Unity-fake, and considered in Synods and Councils; we find several *Canons* or Rules, prescribing concerning Discipline and Penance, wherein it was provided, that Persons notoriously wicked should be removed from the Communion of Christians, and in case of their committing great Sins, inconsistent altogether with the Christian Faith and Hope, utterly excluded and cut off from the Church, and not to be restored, untill after Submission to Penance, which was, such Acts

of

of Humiliation, Mortification, Self-denial, and Charity, as were thought useful to work such Sinners to a true Repentance, and might give ground to the Church to presume that they were in a way of obtaining God's Favour and Mercy for Pardon of their Sins, and so fit to be Reconciled to the Church, and Re-admitted to its Communion, which gave hope of Pardon to Sinners through Christ Jesus. Some of these Canons so Excluded great Sinners, as Apostates, Adulterers, &c. as that they might not be Admitted to the Peace of the Church in a long space of time; some years were required to precede their Reconciliation, and these to be spent in a course of Penance: And in case of Relapse, if any such Penitents fell into the same, or a like grievous Crime the second time, they required such should do Penance until Death. In the Re-admission of Penitents, the Ancient Church was always very careful that its Discipline had its effect to make the Sinner Penitent, as also desirous to discharge the Obligation it saw it self to lie under, of not warranting forgiveness of Sin, but upon due grounds. Upon this Account (according to the Practice) it concerned the Penitent in the first place to make suit to be Admitted, and to declare himself Sorry for,

for, and Offended at himself for what he had done, before he could obtain of the Church to be Admitted to his Penance. Which being granted, and he having undertaken the Penance impofed upon him; in the next place he was Admitted to the Prayers of the Church (at all the Solemn Affemblies of the Church during the time of his Penance) with Impofition of hands, as the mean to obtain Pardon at God's hands; for Impofition of hands in the Ancient Practice was not the Abfolution of the Penitent, but the way to it, and capacity of it, fignifying the Church's Prayer, for the time that fuch continued in doing their Penance, for God's Blefling upon the Means in ufe, to work in them a fincere Repentance, and that fo it would pleafe God to pardon their Sin. And thus the time of the Penance being compleated, the Sinner being fuppofed a true Convert, was reftored to Communion with the Church in the Sacrament of the Eucharift. The ground of this feems to me well expreffed in the Words of *S. Cyprian,* (though upon an occafion different) *Quà fidei & veritati præfumus, eos qui ad fidem & veritatem veniunt & agentes Pænitentiam remitti fibi peccata poftulant, decipere non debemus & fallere : Sed correctos à nobis ac reformatos ad regnum Cælorum Difciplinis cæleftibus cælestibus erudire. We that are over the Faith and Truth, must not deceive those that come to the Faith and Truth, and during Penance, desire their Sins to be remitted: But instruct them, amended and reformed by us, to the Kingdom* of Heaven, *with Heavenly Discipline.* The Church being entrusted with the power of Discipline, for bringing Sinners to Repentance, might neither deceive them nor betray its Trust; but must see therefore that end obtained, the Repentance of the Sinner wrought, and the sincerity of that his Repentance evident after a manner, before it might restore such to Communion with the Church. This produced, tho *Canons* fixing a time for Penance, as also the Rules, assigning several places or stations for the Penitents, in which they were to testify their Repentance, and so by passing through them one after another be reconciled by degrees, into the Church. And the only reason of this strictness being to obtain the End of Discipline, that is, the Sinner's Repentance, and to secure the Church from Guilt, as to God, from which it could not be free in his sight, should it be guilty of so great a fault in its Ministry, as to restore to the Communion of the Church, any that it should not first have Instructed, and wrought to Repentance.

There-

Therefore, many times when Penitents demonstrated a more than ordinary Zeal and eagerness, in detesting the Offences thro' which they had failed, or in taking revenge upon themselves for their Transgressions; or did some eminent act of Piety which testified the sincerity of their Conversion, and gave ground to the Church thereby, to think them qualified for Remission of Sin as to God; the Regular time of their Penance was abated; upon the same consideration as I said before, the Time for Persons continuing in the Rank or State of Catechumens was shortned and Baptism granted, when the Church had ground to presume of their sincerity in the Profession then to be made. Thus in this case the Discipline of Penance being to no other purpose, than to oblige Sinners to take that Course, whereby they may appear to the Church qualified for Remission of Sin; this once appearing, the consideration thereof so took place with the Church, as that the Severity of its Discipline was abated upon it. Insomuch that those strict Canons that enjoined so many Years of Penance for divers great Sins, seem to have been but Threatnings, inviting Sinners to shew that Zeal in Conversion from Sin, as that the Church might have cause to be satisfied of their inward Repentance.   M   This

The Church of England's Wish.

This being the Practice, and this the Aim of Penance in the Primitive Church; let any Man now compare this the Original and general Practice of the Church, with that which we have in the Apostles writings pointed out unto us; and say, by the agreement, whether their Authority were the beginning of it or not. Say, how a Practice so correspondent in all its parts should have been in the Church otherwise: How it should fall out that the Scriptures considered by us should so exactly point out the Primitive Discipline, unless the Apostles had taken order for it in the Churches of their planting, and from thence it continued afterwards: How the same Discipline should prevail through the whole Church; insomuch that there was no Church but what had a Discipline of Penance, and all Churches agreed in its use and design to one purpose, but that it was understood the Church stood charged with the Ministry of this Discipline from Christ and his Apostles, and was obliged to make use of its Power in Christ against such, as having undertaken to live after Christianity when they were Baptized, failed of that undertaking, and departed from that Holy Profession, upon the account of which they were first admitted to be Members of Christ's Church:

How

How it should happen, that the only difference which was in the primitive Church
about Penance, as to the reconciling of
some Sins great and heinous, should fall
out to be in an instance where the strictness of the Apostles Rules obliging the
Church to make difficulty of re-admitting
such Sinners, and S. *Paul*'s own example,
neverthelefs abating of that strictness, in a
particular case, upon his receiving satisfaction of the Sorrow and Repentance of
the Guilty Person, seem at first sight to be
contradictory to each other, so as the
former to give advantage to one Party in
the Dispute, and the latter to the other;
and that these Scriptures should be alledged on either side, and allowed to refer
to the matter of Penance, and that Pardon which the Church might or ought to
give or not give, only the Church that
was in the right, excepting that the Scriptures alledged by the contrary Party, ser-
ved not to prove what they would have;
but that the Church might follow, S. *Paul*'s
example, on like certain evidence of the
Sinner's *Sorrow to Repentance*, and provided the Church took a due care to
bring the Sinner to that Sorrow and Repentance, and to make him sincere therein :
How all this should come to pass, but
that the Church understood the Apostles

in thefe Scriptures, as referring to the
Practice of the Church in their time, and
that their Orders and their Practice were
a Rule for the Church to follow in all
times, according as the fame should appear
in the Scriptures or otherwise; and fo
this difpute fell out to be in a cafe where
the Apoftles Rules and Practice feemed
not fo clear; 'till the Reafon of the cafe
came into confideration; which was this,
that there ought to be difficulty in the
Church's re admitting of fuch Sinners;
becaufe fo great Sins are not without difficulty repented of, the Mind and Confcience of fuch Sinners being depraved, and
defiled in an extraordinary manner; but
neverthelefs Repentance being poffible,
fuppofing it once to be, and that the
Church took fure care to bring it to pafs,
S. *Paul*'s Example might be followed, in
abatement of the ftrictnefs of the Rule.

There is one Thing more in the Primitive Practice of Penance, which I muft
not omit to take notice of (becaufe there
may be occafion to make fome ufe of it,
when we fhall have under confideration
the Benefit and Advantages of Difcipline).
It is this, That Private Perfons, (difcern-
ing what great benefit redounded to the
Penitents, by their being inftructed by
the Church to Repentance, in the time of
their

their Penance; and finding their own Conciences burdened with the like Sins, which being carried in Secrecy, were not subject to the Censures of the Church) were wont therefore, as well for the subduing of the Stubbornels of their hard Hearts, and the furthering their deeper Humiliation, as for the assuring themselves of the sincerity of their Repentance, and obtaining thereby quiet of Mind and peace of Conscience, to Submit themselves to the Church's Discipline herein, and undergo the burden of publick Confession and Penance, when it was thought necessary by him to whom such secret Faults were first discover'd, that they should be brought to the publick notice of the Church, and that the Church's Direction in the Penance, and the Prayers thereof were the best Remedy for the Cure. And we find *Tertullian*, in his Book *de Pœnitentia* very earnest in persuading Christians, of their own Will to undergo this Penance, and *Cyprian, Origen,* and others advising to bring their Secret Sins to the Church for Cure. It seems as tho' there were ground for this Practice in the Direction that S. *James* gives, that the *Sick* should send for the *Elders of the Church to Pray over them,* promising forgiveness of Sins upon their Prayers; from which course, if Benefit might be expected in dan-

M 3 ger

ger of Death, much more in time of Health.
That Apostle indeed, when he proceedeth to
say, *Confess your Sins to one another, and
Pray for one another,* may be understood to
direct our confessing our Sins to one another as well as to the Priests of the Church;
but this is on a supposition, that the cure
of sin is known to all Christians, that God,
who is offended thereby, must be sought
to for Pardon, and that his Pardon is not
to be obtained but by a serious Humiliation and a sincere Repentance; and as a
Man that has no Trouble, nor Guilt of
Conscience upon him, may be better able
to advise one under such circumstances,
than he to advise himself, so the Skill and
Fidelity of a private Christian may Furnish
his Brother with a good Cure for his Sin,
by putting him in the way of Repentance,
and he may by his Prayers be assisting to
him also therein; which may be a good
reason why Christians should confess their
faults one to another, in respect of benefit
which they may have from this, and why
it should be enjoyned as it is by S. *Paul* on
private Christians, to *restore* him that is
surprized in Sin; and yet all this shall
afford a greater Reason, why Confession
of our Secret Sins should be made to the
Church, and offered to the Cure of the
more skilful Physician, the Church being
best

beſt able to direct us in the way of Repentance, and its Prayers prevalent with God beyond the Prayers of a private Brother, as this alſo may much better aſſure us of the ſincerity of our Repentance, and give greater comfort to our Minds after we have gone through the courſe appointed for our obtaining God's Pardon, and as in every reſpect, the operation and effect of God's Miniſtry in the Church muſt be accounted greater than that which a private Chriſtian may do for the good of Souls. But this however ſeems to have been good Advice, and not Precept, for that a Man's own Skill and Fidelity to his own Salvation may poſſibly furniſh him his Cure at home; in which reſpect there's no neceſſity for a Man to confeſs his Sin to his Brother, though it may be of good uſe to him, nor to the Church, though that be certainly of more. The Obligation that lieth upon a Sinner to this purpoſe being ſuch as doth not ſuppoſe, but that his Sin may poſſibly be cured otherwiſe;and yet, that it may beſt, and moſt effectually be cured by the Miniſtry of God's Church. So that it lyeth upon the Conſcience before God, that ſuch an one both know that which muſt be done in the Work of Repentance, and voluntarily charge himſelf with that Humiliation which may

M 4

Mor-

Mortify in himſelf thoſe Paſſions and Luſts that cauſed him to Sin afore, and make his Profeſſion ſincere for the future; and therein ſupply to himſelf the Work and Effect of the Church's Miniſtry: or that he ſeek to that Miniſtry which God has provided, to cleanſe and cure his Sin.

But I return to conſider the proof that has been made of a Diſcipline in the Church, obliging Chriſtians to a courſe of Repentance for their known Tranſgeſſions; being that which hath ſhewn them what lieth upon themſelves to do, that they may get clear of Guilt lying upon their Conſciences for ſecret Sins; but which God hath appointed to be executed by the Miniſters of his Church, to conſtrain them to Penance for ſuch Sins as they are known to have committed, contrary to their Duty as Chriſtians, and to the good Profeſſion they made when they were firſt admitted into the Church of Chriſt. Now the proof given is a connection of Arguments that take hold of, and are linked one into the other ſo cloſe and firm, that they hold or break altogether. It hath been ſhewn, That the Inſtitution of Diſcipline is from Chriſt, who gave Power and Authority for that purpoſe to his Church, under the Figure of the Keys, for the opening a Door in his House,

House, to Let in and Admit fuch, as defired, and would make themfelves fit for Admiffion thereinto; and for the fhutting that Door againft others, that muft be removed and put forth thence, (nothing being to be fuffered to abide therein, as nothing to enter that defileth). And that the Opening and giving Admittance into the Church of Chrift implying an Admittance to the Hope of God's Pardon as to our Sins; and on the other hand, the Shutting out and Excluding from the Church of Chrift implying an Exclufion, and Shutting out from the hope of God's Promifes, in that refpect, the Effect of the ufe of the Keys in the way of Difcipline, which removeth Notorious Sinners from the Houfe and Church of God, and refufeth to Re-admit them till their Repentance appear, is very properly exprefs'd in that, which according to our Saviour's Intent, fhould be the Effect of the Power of the Keys given to his Church, Namely, the *Binding* and *Loofing,* and *Remitting* and *Retaining Sins.* As alfo, That our Saviour's Words, *Tell the Church,* and the Obligation therein prefumed on all to *hear the Church,* as to what this might Admonifh them about their Faults, and the further implication of that which the Church muft proceed to in *Binding* or *Loofing,* according

according as Men shall *hear or not hear* the
Church, in reference to what may have
been done by them contrary to their Duty
as Christians, do certainly shew a Power
lodged in the Church, to take Cognisance
of what Men may do contrary to their
Duty, and a necessity of Submission to the
Church's Authority, in *hearing* what that
shall think fit to Direct or Admonish thereupon; and that Mens Sins are bound upon them, if the Church shall proceed to
Censure their Crimes, because it cannot
prevail with them to amend. And, That
the Practice of the Apostles making use
of their Power in Christ to this purpose,
and the Orders, which it appears by several Passages of Scripture they took with
the Churches of their Planting to Act accordingly, that is to say, to call the Professors of Christianity to Account for
what should be done by them contrary
to that Profession ; to Admonish, Rebuke,
and Reprove their Faults; to Remove,
and put away from the Church of God,
the Disobedient and Disorderly; are both
an Argument that they understood our
Lord Christ to have given his Church a
Power of this nature. as also, a sufficient
Precedent to the Church of Christ to Act
upon the same Power for the same Puposes
in all times. It hath been also shewn,
what

what the Practice of Discipline was in the Time of the Apostles, and in the Churches of their Planting; and that the Apostles both informed the Churches of their Power in Christ for this purpose, and gave charge concerning the same. As also, that the Discipline of the Church in the Primitive time was in all respects correspondent to that, which appear'd to be the Practice of the Apostles, and of their Order: The Primitive Church, which being nearest the Fountain, is to be supposed to have best understood the meaning of the Scriptures, either thence deriving the Grounds and Method of that Discipline which it Exercised, or, as I rather think, Regulating its Practice, (which had its beginning from Tradition, and Unwritten Orders of the Apostles, left with the several Churches of their Planting) according to that which appear'd in their Writings concerning their Practice or Orders about this Matter.

If therefore any Man shall go about to overthow this Proof; it shall not be enough to do it, that he can put another sense upon the Words of our Saviour, which we have supposed to be the foundation of the Church's Power in this case, but he must shew that they are not capable of being understood in the sense that hath here been
pleaded

pleaded for; and that the Apostles and
the Churches of their time, acting according to such a Power as hath been supposed
given by our Saviour therein, is nothing
of an Argument why we should so understand them.   Nor shall it suffice to advance some other meaning of those Texts
cited out of S. *Paul's,* and the other E-
pistles, unless that meaning be free
from contradiction, and unless it can be
shewn withal that those Scriptures have
no intent to speak of, or refer to Discipline
or Penance in the Church, and that no such
then were. For otherwise, admitting Discipline and Penance to have been, there will be
no reason but to suppose an intent in the
Scriptures to speak of it, and then the
agreement in this meaning of the Scriptures to Historical Truth, will justify it,
even to common Sense: Nor shall it be
enough to say, that Ecclesiastical Discipline came to effect in the Primitive Church
by the consent of Christians, at a time
when the Church wanted the Assistance of
the Civil Magistrate. For this is presumption enough, that it was not only the
Consent of Christians that gave beginning
to it. That we find no beginning of that
Consent among the Churches, yet find
that in all Churches there was a Discipline; And therefore 'tis reasonable to
think

think it must have been from the Apostles,
otherwise it would not have been universal. And when we see such hints of, and
references to, yea, and Orders concerning it in their Writings, and the Primitive
Church understanding these Texts of Scripture to this purpose, and Appealing to
them in Vindication of its Practice, I do
not perceive it can be made a Question,
whether the Primitive Church received it
from them. It was indeed the Consent of
Christians that gave Effect to the Discipline of the Church in those Times, but
admitting the Apostles to have taken Order for it in the Churches, and Christ to
have given his Church a Power for this
purpose, they could not have been Christians, had they not consented and con-
curred with the Church, for bringing it
to Effect. The Church, its true, in the
beginning, had no Favour nor Protection
from the Civil Powers; but I see not wherein it can be pretended, that its Discipline
was appointed for that reason. The only
thing that can be offered towards it, is,
that the *Jews* devised first Excommunication after their Captivity, making use
thereof in their dispersion, while they
were under Foreign Powers, not having
any Precept for it in the Law of *Moses.*
And this I take to be True, that the *Jews*
(desiring

(defiring, as they ought, to maintain God's Law, by which they were to be Governed, but not having the power of inflicting Penalties requifite to maintain it, after their own Civil Government was deftroyed) devifed this Courfe, as feeming to them reafonable and neceffary, that fuch as would not obferve the Law, fhould be deprived of the priviledge of a *Jew,* and fhut out from the Converfation of his Native People, either in whole, or in part, according as hisOffence was. But neverthelefs, it is not to be thought, but that this came in force in the Church by the Act of our Lord Chrift and his Apoftles, Founding his Church, and giving it this Power, and requiring it to be put in Practice, this appearing in the Scriptures of the New Teftament, and an Alteration alfo appearing as to the Ufe and Defign of Excommunication, which among the *Jews* was a Civil Penalty only, but in the *Chriftian Church* ferveth to Spiritual purpofes. Well and good it may be thought, that there being a Cuftom of this Nature in the Synagogue, our Saviour Chrift framing his Church as near as might be to the pattern of the Synagogue, preferving the difference between the Spiritual and Legal Service of God, appointed therefore a like Proceeding, for to keep Chriftians within the Bounds of their

their Duty, but giving Power from God, to make the Discipline of his Church Effectual beyond that of the *Jews*, and to serve more Spiritual Ends: as he was pleased to do in another case; namely, in Appointing Baptism, (which was a Ceremony used by the *Jews* in their Admission of Proselytes of the *Gentiles*, to Live among them and resort to their Temple for the Worship of the God of *Israel*) to be a Rite in his Church, for the Admission of such as desired to be Members thereof, but this, with power from himself making it of another Effect, and to serve other more Spiritual purposes than the *Jews* used, or pretended it for. So that though Excommunication were only of Humane Institution among the *Jews*, and designed to serve a present Turn, and supply their not having power to Execute the Law of *Moses* whilst they were dispersed among other Nations, and whilst they were under the Government of Strangers in their own Land; it shall not thence follow, that Excommunication is no other in the Church of Christ, nor that it was taken up for no other purpose, and must be laid aside when the occasion of that purpose ceaseth: But as it had its beginning in the Church from our Lord Christ and his Apostles, so that which may appear of their purpose

in

in doing it, shall determine its use in the Christian Church and its continuance shall be necessary as long as these purposes remain, to which it may be useful.

CHAP. VI.

HERE is the place for me to take notice of the usefulness of Discipline in the Church of Christ, and of that Power and Authority which Excludeth Sinners from it. Now there can be no doubt of the usefulness hereof in any Man that rightly considers the Ends designed therein, and looks upon it as sufficient for the accomplishment of those Ends? There be many I know in the World, who finding not the Church endued with any Temporal Power, to enforce by way of Constraint, that Discipline it pretendeth to Exercise, or those Censures which pass therein against Offenders, do for that very Reason think and speak Contemptuously of this Institution of the Gospel; But a True Christian, that looketh upon our Lord Christ as having power over the Souls and Consciences of Men, will think him able to give Power and Efficacy to this as

well

well as other Spiritual Institutions of his Gospel, when Administred in his Name, and according to his Mind and Will, though the Power thereof being Spiritual, appear not to us in the way of its Operation, but only as when the Effect is wrought, it appeareth to have had its Operation on the Consciences of Men by the Power of Christ. It was on this Account that S. *Paul* 1 *Cor.* 10. 4. Speaking of the Power and Authority of his Apostleship, and the Instruments of his Ministry acting against sin and sinners, saith, *The Weapons of our Warfare are not Carnal, but Mighty through God, to the pulling down of Strong Holds, casting down Imaginations, and every high thing, that exalteth it self against the knowledge of God, and bringing into Captivity every thought to the Obedience of Christ* : that is, The Discipline and Censures of the Church are not Weak and Contemptible, but Mighty, such as have a Force, through the Power of God upon the Conscience, for the Beating down all the Fortifications which Sin may have Raised in Men's Hearts to Defend it self there, and Subduing the most Refractory Offenders. Let Credit be given to S. *Paul* in this which he saith of this Act of the Ministry, that it is *Mighty through God,* a Divine Force accompanying it to render it Effectual up-

N

on

on Men's Consciences, and the usefulness therof cannot but appear from the Ends designed it in the Church of Christ, and its effectually serving those Ends, indeed the necessity of it will hence appear. Among the known Ends of Discipline in the Church the principal is the bringing of Sinners to Repentance, and to this End, of all the Means in the Gospel Ministry, this is the most Efficacious. *Preaching* may shew Men the guilt of Sin, and convince them, that without Repentance and Conversion, there is no Remission of Sin, nor hope of Everlasting Life: yet whilst Sinners are suffered to live in the Society of the Faithful, and left to themselves to set upon the Work of Repentance at their own time, and to satisfie themselves only as to their sincerity therein, it is to be feared, they may endeavour to Reconcile the Hopes of Heaven with the Enjoyment of their Lusts; they may not be very strict in searching into themselves and their hearts, touching the sincerity of their Conversion, nor very severe upon themselves in taking Revenge upon themselves for that wherein they may have presumptuously sinned; But being admitted to the same privileges with other Members of the Church, may presume on God's Grace and Mercy; and though they continue in Sin,

Sin, think neverthelefs that they are as good Chriftians, and have as much right to Salvation as others, which is a moft dangerous, but withal, a moft common Imagination. But when Difcipline and the Power which God hath given the Church over them that Tranfgrefs the Profeffion of Chriftianity after they have made it, fhall be employed to procure the Repentance of Sinners, to conftrain them to a courfe that may be effectual to Repentance; to inftruct them in the work, and by meet helps forward them in it, or Exclude them the Communion of the Church if they refufe it, and therein difallow their Hopes, and pretenfions to God's Favour and Mercy, forafmuch as they have departed from that Profeffion which is the ground of a Chriftian's Confidence in God through Jefus Chrift: Men muft be very much hardned in Sin, if when the Church *Rebukes them with Authority,* they will not be Reclaimed; if they refufe the courfe of Repentance when they fee they fhall *not be fpared,* but that the Church hath power *in readinefs to Revenge their Difobedience,* as S. *Paul's* Expreffion is; or at leaft, if when the Church fhall not think fit to allow them to partake with other Chriftians in the Sacrament that affures the Benefits of Chrift, they become not hence concerned

to

to affure and recover by repentance their hope in him ; efpecially if finding themfelves under the Power of Satan, by being caft out of the Church of Chrift, his Terror, the Terror of their own Circumftances, and the Terrors of the Lord, have not an influence on their Minds, fo as to occafion their Sorrowing unto Repentance. It was this Sorrow, even fuch as produced Repentance to Salvation, according to God, wrought by the Cenfure inflicted on the Inceftuous Perfon at *Corinth* by S. *Paul's* Epiftle. And 'tis reafonable to think, that the Repentance of Sinners will, in likelihood be more fincere and durable by their going through the prefcribed Penance, and having not only the Inftructions, but Prayers alfo of the Church to affift them, and obtain the affiftances of God's Spirit for them, to make their Repentance Effectual. It is not every one that is fenfible what meafure of Humiliation and Mortification is neceffary to Subdue the Corruptions and Lufts of a Heart defperately wicked, nor is it every one that knows it, that will of himfelf undergo that Humiliation and Mortification that is neceffary : But the courfe of Humiliation, which the Church prefcribeth, humbleth the Hearts of Sinners, that they repent with perfect Repentance. There are

are not many that think it a difficulty to
recover the Favour of God after wilful
Sins, nor that are apprehensive that there
is difficulty for a Man to assure himself,
that the resolution of his Heart to live after God's Will for the future is sincere, or
will be effectual and durable : But when the
Discipline of the Church removeth those
Sinners from the Church that visibly fail
of the Profession made at their Baptism,
and maketh difficulty to Re-admit them,
till they shall have given satisfaction of
the sincerity of their Repentance; this
must shew Sinners that they are not lightly
to presume for the pardon of those Sins,
which the Church can hardly presume that
a Man can repent him of enough; and
that the renewing the Heart to a sincere
and lasting Resolution of this kind is no
easie nor slight Work, which the Ministry
of the Church has so much ado to bring
about, by a long and strict course of Penance. Besides, Discipline in the Church
is useful to more than those upon whom
it is immediately exercised. S. *Paul* intimates to *Timothy,* that if they that sin are
Rebuked before all, others *will fear* to sin in
like manner; will have fear also in respect
of their secret Sins, which being known
to God and their own Consciences they cannot hope will be remitted, unless they

forth-

forthwith betake themselves to that Repentance which the Church, concerned for the Salvation of Souls, would put them to, in case their Sins were known. It was this fear that put so many good Christians heretofore upon bringing their secret Sins to the Church for Cure, for their being better assisted in the Work of Repentance, not having reason to think, (upon so good grounds as the safety of the Soul requires) that they could of themselves perform the Work of Repentance effectually without that help which the Ministry of God's Church might furnish. And if the same fear do not again prevail, whenever Discipline shall come in use in the Church, to make Men seek the Ministry of the Church in respect of their secret Sins ; it will at least make every one concerned, voluntarily to charge himself with that Humiliation that may mortify Sin in himself, and work such a change in his heart, that the same shall for the future detest and hate Sin, as much, and more than it formerly loved it ; inasmuch as otherwise a Man cannot assure himself of God's Pardon, seeing the Church will not become the Warrant of it to any but those that its Ministry hath wrought to use the necessary means of Repentance. Moreover, Discipline is useful and necessary for the Church

in

in General, to keep all the Members of the Church in the way of their Duty, to preserve the Body pure, and likewise clear from Scandal; for both the Church and the Ministry thereof cannot be clear from Scandal if there be not a Discipline, therein to reprove, Rebuke, and put away, if need be, Notorious Sinners from the Communion of the Church. The Honour of the Christian Religion always suffereth, when the Professors thereof live in Unrighteousness: The Honour of the Church as a Society must therefore suffer, if being constituted a Society, to promote God's Service and the things that appertain to Godliness, it shall do nothing as a Church, to restrain the Wickedness of Men. Its Ministry also must lie under Reproach as tho' it were a Ministry of Sin, if the Church be remiss in Discipline: for how faithfully soever the Truth of Christ be Preached according to the Tenour of his Commission, that *Repentance and Remission of Sins should be Preached in his Name,* the former as of absolute Necessity in them that would assure their hope of the latter; yet if the Church in Ministring the Sacraments, which are means of assuring and confirming the hope of Christians as to the Remission of their Sins, shall not concern it self to discern how fit they are for them,

N 4 that

that pretend to them; as also to procure
that disposition which maketh Men capable of forgiveness; refusing those that are
visibly not qualified by Repentance, as
its Ministry in this respect is by no means
trustily discharged; so it giveth but too
great advantage to Sinners to presume on
God's Mercy upon undue grounds, and
bringeth blame on the Ministry, as giving
countenance and encouragement to them,
and Sinners. So that the Honour of Religion, and of the Church of God, and
the Reputation of its Ministry will all
suffer through the neglect of Discipline.

And yet alas! this Discipline, though
(as hath been proved) of Divine Institution, having its beginning from the express Laws of Christ and his Apostles;
though observed with all strictness in the
Primitive and Apostolical Church; though
given in Charge as a part of the Ministry
by the Apostles, and in it self most necessary, in respect of such as may have Er-
red from the Truth and Righteousness, to
restore them and save their Souls from Death,
even effectual to instruct them in Repentance unto Life; though also in its own
nature of absolute use to preserve Religion in its Purity; is nevertheless in the
present state of the Church discontinued
and in a manner wholly disregarded, as
though

though it never had been mentioned in that Scripture which we acknowledge for the Rule of Religion. And though the want of Discipline be an Evil that may be felt in the great Loosness and Irregularity of the Manners of Christians, yet the Remedy is not looked after. There were Abuses its true, crept into the Discipline of the Church, even such as made that Discipline not effectual to the Purposes of its Institution; but the Question is, whether those Abuses ought to be removed, and Discipline continued in the Church, or whether this be to be set aside wholly for the sake of those. I am perswaded, if the things be true, that have been premised upon grounds from Scripture, and the Practice of the Primitive Church, touching the Original Institution, and concerning also the Ends of Discipline and its Use in the Church of Christ, the Reformation of the Church consists in retaining Discipline, and by removal of Abuses, restoring it to its right use in the Church of Christ.

But before I come to press this home upon those whom it will concern, I think it expedient to take notice of the decay of Discipline in Christ's Church, and the Abuses crept into its Practice; for that will shew us what the Discipline of Christ's Church

Church would be, Abufes and Corruptions fet afide, and what it fhould be reftored to be.   Now it hath been made appear already in this Difcoufe, that in time
of the Apoftles and firft Ages of the Church
fucceeding them, there was a ftrict Difci-
cipline obferved and practifed in the Church
to hold men to their Chriftian Profeffion,
and put thofe, who contrary to the Profeffion they had made to God and his
Church fell into Sins deftructive to Chriftianity, under Penance, or in cafe they
were Refractory under Cenfure, fo that
they flood deprived of the Communion of
the Church, till they had given fatisfaction of their being more fincere in Chriftianity.   The Piety and Zeal of Chriftians abating , the ftrictnefs of Difcipline
abated alfo by degrees from age to age,
till that now it is come almoft to nothing.
There probably might be fome Remiffnefs
in it, at the time when *Montanus,* and *Tertullian* who followed him, pretended it not
to be in the power of the Church to allow
Penance, being the means of Reconciliation to great Sins.   Not that I think *Montanus* and his followers were in the right,
in difallowing the Church's Power to re-
leafe any fort of Sinners from Cenfure
when their Repentance fhould be manifeft.
But the Scruples which feveral Churches
had

had in this matter, (who though they did not break Communion as *Montanus* and his Followers, yet were not eafily brought to reft fatisfied in what other Churches did in reconciling great Sins, fearing prejudice to Religion from the grant of Reconciliation to fuch) feems to me an argument that there was a flackening or fome abatement of Difcipline at that time ; a fear there plainly was of fome fuch thing. And as men are apt when Difputes arife to run into extremes, either thinking to make their caufe the better by it, or better to ferve their private ends thereby ; fo hence *Montanus* and his Followers might take occafion to depart from the Church, and raife their own Reputation under pretence of maintaining the ftrict Difcipline of Chrift's Church, and for this purpofe infift on fuch a rigor of Difcipline as appeared fpecious indeed becaufe pretended to deter from Sin ; but yet different from the Difcipline of Chrift, which being intended to bring Sinners to Repentance, when that end is obtained , may and ought by the Church to be releafed. On the other hand there is fome probability , that notwithftanding the Church took care (having afferted its power of readmitting the greateft Sinners to its Communion by the means of Penance) to provide that fuch Sinners fhould should perform their Penance before they were restored thereto, for that otherwise the Church must have betrayed her Trust in allowing the hopes of God's Pardon to such as were not qualified for it according to the Gospel of Christ ; yet there might be ill men that took advantage hence (as such do not unusually even abuse the Mercy of God to wicked purposes) to allow themselves the more liberty to do Wickedly upon the account that the greatest of Sinners though excluded the Communion of the Church for their Crimes, might nevertheless be readmitted to it upon Penance : Not that these thought of performing their Penance according to the Order of the Church, any more than such think of Repenting for their Sins in the manner that God requireth (which is with true contrition of Heart) when they abuse the Divine Mercy and Sin upon presumption thereof ; but such most likely had Thoughts of doing no more Penance than pleased themselves , or standing it out with the Church should a severe Penance be put upon them ; or it may be, they valued not Communion with the Church in the Sacrament of the Eucharist, which would not suffer them to be easy in their Sins, but thought they might live more at Ease and at their Liberty in the state of Peni-

Penitents, having privilege of being present at some parts of the Worship, and
being allowed the Communion at their
Death, or in danger of Death. Not that
the Church in allowing the Communion to
those that were in the state of Penitents
in danger of Death, or in admitting to
Penance upon Confession in these circumstances, and granting thereupon the Communion of the Church, did act therein
contrary to the Discipline of Christ;
for that the Church supposed such in the
way of Penance and Repentance, and had
reason to think God would accept the
Disposition, where he gave not time to
fulfill the work; and besides, the Communion was given provisionally as well to
obtain the Grace of God to strengthen the
Penitent in that exigent, as for the quiet
of his Conscience; and withal the party
stood bound to perform the Penance which
was or should be enjoined, in case he Recovered: And if such survived not to
perform their Penance, their Salvation remained questionable with the Church.
So that the Communion was not refused to
such Sinners, in regard it was possible, that
the Sorrow wherewith they submitted to
Penance in that case might be so sincere as
to obtain pardon at God's hands; but in
regard of the Doubt that remained in the
busi-

business, there was question made of the
Salvation of such as were prevented by
Death from making it appear that they
were truly converted. Hitherto the Church
was not faulty in its Discipline, but some
false Christians abused its good Orders,
and found means of evading and eluding
its Discipline. Such were those that S. *Cyprian*
finds fault with, that put the Martyrs upon demanding their being restored to the
Church before the time for their Penance
was expired. The case was this, the
Order of the Church always allowed an
Abatement of Penance enjoined, upon appearance of extraordinary Zeal or Piety,
such as might be a presumption that a true
Conversion was wrought; upon this account if any shewed so great a Zeal for
Christianity as to suffer or run the hazard
of suffering for the Truth, this was satisfaction to the Church, so that there was
an end of their Penance, and they had free
admission to the Communion thereof.
And the Church having the Zeal and Holiness of Martyrs and Confessors in esteem,
did thereupon encline to favour in some
respect such Friends of theirs as they in-
terceeded for, in the Abatement of their
Penance according to the strict Rules of
the Church, and granting them the Communion of the Church the sooner, because
those

those Persons had a good Opinion of them as to their being sincere in their Repentance. But hence arose a very great abuse to the abatement of the strictness of Discipline in the Church and to the hazard of many Souls. For Offenders hereupon applied to the Martyrs and Confessors to demand on their behalf the Communion of the Church and the taking off their Penance; which *Cyprian* finds fault with as a Seditious practice, tending to destroy and subvert the whole Discipline of the Church, and to frustrate its whole design for the good of Souls: and therefore denies it to be in the Power of Confessors to grant such Indulgences as they pretended to, and that the Church ought to oppose them therein and not suffer it. By this means the Church kept up its Discipline as yet: However Corruption and Wickedness still growing more and more among the Professors of Christianity; those that made Profession of it, many of them became loose in their Lives, and were unwilling to hazard much for the sake of their Profession; so that in the latter Persecutions great multitudes fell away and committed Idolatry with the Gentiles, and those the Persecutions being over, were willing to return again to the Church, but not willing to submit to the Rules of its Discipline, which   and

and therefore made Parties and Factions in the Church to get themselves received, and by their multitude as well as other not warrantable means got to be received, and the course of Penance according to the Rules of the Church not to be infifted on. Had the Church complied with these of choice, it had been the betraying of its Truft in the Miniftry; but complying and condefcending as it did only to avoid a further Inconvenience or Mifchief, that is to fay, Schifm or a breach in the Church, of all things moft prejudicial to the general good of the Body, there could hereupon be no juft caufe for the Blame which the *Novatians* laid on the Church upon this Account; nor could it be underftood that the Church warranted Forgivenefs of Sins to thofe, whom fhe received after this manner, further than that Difpofition of Mind, which the Parties themfelves they returned with, might warrant inafmuch as it was evident that the Church waved the Rule, by which it was proceed, for to prevent the mifchief of a Schifm, in that refpect the Charge of making good that Difpofition, which qualified before God for the Communion of the Church, muft devolve upon the Confciences of thofe that impofed the neceffity upon the Church to wave thofe wholefome some Rules. And upon this ground the Answer in defence of the Church against the *Novatians* was, That *if any did deceive the Church with the semblance of Repentance, God (who is not mocked and who beholdeth the Heart of Man) may judge of these things which his Servants did not well discern, and the Lord may amend the Sentence of his Servants,* and punish the Iniquities of such notwithstanding their Reconciliation with the Church. Besides even at that time, unless where the Church was under a necessity aforesaid through Faction or fear of Schism, Persons were not presently admitted to Penance and the Communion, but this was done as a Writer of that time says, *With great pondering of the matter and with great deliberation, after many Sighs and shedding of Tears, after the Prayers of the whole Church.* The breach therefore was not so great upon the Discipline of the Church, but that the strictness of Discipline was in some measure restored afterwards, and Reconciliation not granted to every one that would ask it, but upon evidence of their being greatly affected with the sense of their Sins, and upon their submission to the Order of the Church.

But in some time after this, great Disorders began to break in upon the Church, the

The Church of England's *Wish.*

Civil Powers becoming Chriftian, a mix'd Multitude came into the Church, for the fake of Worldly Priviledges, not for the fake of Religion; and after this Scandals were foon multiply'd in that Body, which had been formerly remarkable for the Purity of their Morals, and Strictnefs of their Lives. And now began the Corruption of Difcipline: Many Profeffed Chriftianity, either for Fashion-fake, or for hope of Advantage, but the greater part of thefe came not with a Refolution to live according to it, neither would they be brought to do it; by this means Offenders were too numerous and too headftrong for the Difcipline of the Church to hold them in Compafs: Even the Clergy were Corrupted by, and with the People, infomuch that fome of them abufed their Power in Chrift, *Lording it over God's Heritage,* and making ufe of the Authority, that fhould have been employed againft Vice and Wickednefs, and for the bringing Sinners to Repentance, to Subject the Vulgar to themfelves, to ferve the Ends of their Ambition, and to execute fometimes, even their Malice and Revenge. Factions alfo were common among the People, to exempt Offenders from Cenfure, and from Penance, and the Lewdnefs of Chriftians encreafed to that Degree, that the World
coming

coming into the Church, was said to be
the decay of Christianity, though it en-
creased so greatly the number of Christian
Professors. These Evils, the Church for
some time strugled with, in its Councils and
Synods, making, and setling Rules to bring
both the Clergy and Laity under Discipline,
appointing Censures according to Men's
Crimes, as also the degrees and time of
Penance, and Methods for the Receiving
of Penitents again to the Church; such,
as had they been observed, according to
the intent of those faithful Pastors that
had the Interest and Common Good of
Christianity, and the Reformation of Christians in view in their Establishment of
those Laws; and notice also taken of
what was Spiritual therein; would have
preserved the Discipline of the Church,
and rendred it Effectual to its true Purpose
of making the Lives of Christians answer-
able to their Profession, and Reforming
such things as were amiss amongst them.

But as multiplying of Laws in the Corrupt State of a Commonwealth, is thought
to be a Remedy, and for that purpose usually many Laws are made, yet availeth
little, those that should Execute them being corrupted, and the Corruptions of
Men striving always against the Laws, to
Evade or Elude them, and sometimes to

Bear

Bear them down, or Bear down those that
would uphold the Power of the Laws.
So it was in this Cafe with the Church;
the Clergy being themfelves corrupt, began to neglect their Function, efpecially
this, the moft difficult part of their Miniftry ; relaxed the Difcipline of the Church,
for that the Rigor of it was uneafie to
themfelves ; complyed with Great Men,
who thought it hard to fubmit to the Publick Order ; fought themfelves, ferved
their own Ambition and Paffions by the
Authority they had in Chrift for other
Purpofes, which made their Miniftry Reproached and Contemned : The Body of
the People would not be kept within
Bounds, their Vices were too Numerous
and too Powerful to be controuled, fome
ftood it out with their Paftors, others that
fubmitted to a Penance, did it only in
Formality, not minding the Spiritual intent thereof, nor concerning themfelves
to Sorrow after a Godly fort ; fuch as were
under Cenfure aimed and contended to be
prefently re-admitted to the Church, not
minding to fit themfelves for it, nor content that the Church fhould oblige them
to a courfe that might make them fit by a
True Repentance. Yea, fuch was their
Lewdnefs, that the Difcipline of the Church
came amongft them into Ridicule. The
Sim-

Simplicity and Honefty of many well-meaning Chriftians, who for their Soul's fake, for help in the Work of Repentance and for the quiet of their Confcience, brought their Sins to the Church, and many times, by the direction of their Paftors, made Open and Publick Confeffion of the fame in the Affemblies, defiring the Prayers of the Church to God on their behalf, was Mocked and Laughed at, and fuch things as fhould have been to the Sorrow of all, noted for Sport amongft many, and remembred to the Shame of fuch as were much better Chriftians than thofe that Reproached them. Howbeit, fuch was the Scandal hereby occafioned, that the Church hereupon was forced to alter its Method, and appoint that fecret Sins fhould no more be Confeffed Publickly. This I take to be that which was done by *Nectarius*, who was followed therein, firft, by the Churches of the *Eaft*, and afterwards by thofe in the *Weft*. For we find in the Practice of the Times following, that the Order of Publick Penance was not wholly taken away, but according to the Ancient Difcipline Eftablifhed by the Apoftles in the Church; open Offenders were openly Cenfured, and preffed to make publick Confeffion of their Faults. Neverthelefs there is reafon to think that

this

this very Thing, the Lewdnefs of common
Chriftians Mocking and Infulting at their
Brethrens Simplicity and Devotion when
they made open Confeffion of their Sins
in Penance; did at length create a Prejudice even in the Minds of well-difpofed
Chriftians againft the Order of the Church
in this particular. And of this fo much
advantage was taken by ill men, who before fought by finifter means and Practices to undermine the Difcipline of
the Church, as now openly to ftand out
againft it, and refufe that Confeffion of Sins in Publick, which hitherto
had been not only thought to be the
beft Teftimony of the Converfion of
fuch Siners, but alfo a moft effectual
means of humbling them, and working
thereby their Converfion: This, and feveral finifter practices of Penitents to get
themfelves reftored to the peace of the
Church and fhift their Penance, (in which
fuch Boldnefs was at length ufed, that
what the Church could not yield to with
fafety of Difcipline, Paftors could not refufe well with fafety to themfelves) brought
in a Practice which was the Ruin of the
Order of the Church. Penitents were
fuffered, inftead of the publick Penance,
according to the Ancient courfe of Difcipline, to do it fecretly, in fome private
place,

place, in the presence of a few good Men, and this at the discretion of the Bishop, (or Confessor, in case of private Sins) and Absolution was given also privately. This Temper was found, because the Generality would not submit to setled Rules ; and to let their Sins pass without any Censure, was not thought as yet, a Thing that the Governors of the Church might with a safe Conscience suffer.

But in a little time the Clergy growing Corrupt with the People, to a very great degree, became themselves Corrupters of the People, accepting and allowing Commutations of Penance, taking upon themselves to favour Penitents in the injunction of their Penance, abating therein the Ancient Severities, admitting Rich Men to buy off their Penance under the decenter name of giving Alms, and under pretence of contributing to Devotion, and the Honour of God, in procuring Masses to be said, wherein a secret gain was made by the Managers of the Church's Discipline : Who, willing to serve their Ambitious as well as Covetous Ends, kept up an Opinion among the People, that it was necessary for Men to seek to the Ministry of the Church for the cure of their Sins, but intending to use their Ministry to their own purposes, they laid aside the use

O 4   thereof

thereof to the purposes of Christ; that is to say, the procuring in Sinners that Disposition which might qualify them for God's Pardon and Mercy; and assumed to themselves a Power of giving Pardon in God's stead, of changing also Attrition into Contrition by their Ministry, for this thinking themselves and their Ministry should be more highly valued and esteemed; and to keep their hold of that whereof they made a Profit, the Penance was enjoyned after Absolution, not as having reference to the Pardon of Sin, but as necessary in respect of Temporal Punishment which God might inflict notwithstanding that Pardon which his Ministers had granted. And being for such a purpose, 'twas pretended to be wholly in the Power of the Ministry to enjoyn such satisfactions as they saw cause, yea, to grant satisfactions of others to the account of such as desired them, which at last came to be to those that would pay for them, and so Indulgences were set to open Sale. This Evil we must suppose grew by degrees, from several Changes which the Discipline of the Church suffered through the wickedness of Men. Even after many of the Clergy themselves became Corrupt, perverting and abusing the Discipline of the Church; it is to be supposed, that some used

used the Remains of Discipline to the best purpose they could in the present circumstances, and we must think that the Reason and Faith of many Christians bore up, so as not to be carried away with those Corruptions, to which the Faults and Corruptions of such as Acting in the Church's Ministry abused the same, might give too great occasion. Alms-deeds, as first they were enjoyned in Penance, for that they are contrary to Covetousness and that immoderate desire of Worldly Things, which is the common Temptation Men have to do Evil, as also, for that it must be a sign of Christian Charity in the Heart, when Men Dedicate to Charity those Worldly Goods and Possessions which Unrighteousness doth neither get, nor bestow well; so might be well designed, even when trusted in the hands of the Clergy to be disposed; or when first required to be trusted in their hands for Pious uses. For secret Penance there was a Reason, when the Corruption of the Age would not submit to the better Course; and thereof there might be, and was use and advantage to Christianity, when, and as long as the Pastor was Faithful, and directed to proper means for bringing the Sinner to sincere Repentance. Even the Law of secret Confession to be made once a Year to the Priest, which is now one of the

the most gross Abuses in the Church of *Rome*, was probably made a Law in the Church at first, upon good Reason, and for a good End its likely; because it could not be thought of all Christians, if left to themselves, that they would voluntarily charge themselves with that Humiliation and those Acts of Self-denial as are necessary to work Repentance; that therefore it was made a Law of the Church, that all should bring their Sins to the Church; and because this they would not do publickly, it was on that account thought fit they should do it to Confessors in private; and this to be done once a year, because, if left to themselves for the time, 'twas not likely to be done at all. But these things being an abatement of that Discipline which our Lord and his Apostles Instituted, and consequently an abatement to the Efficacy of his Ordinance; or an Abuse of that Discipline, (for such Alms and Gifts for Pious Uses, as pretended, must be said to be, when accepted in Commutation for Penance, to which they might in some respect have Ministred as Means, but which they set aside, as taken in lieu thereof) and consequently, in no wise serving to the True Ends of that Discipline in the Church; did hereby give advantage to the perverse inclinations of

Men

Men to fruſtrate more and more the Diſcipline of Chriſt's Church, and to ſhelter themſelves and their wicked works from it. And the wickedneſs of Men, accordingly took the Advantage, inſomuch that the Clergy being themſelves Corrupt, began to have no great liking to that Diſcipline which would reform them; and were the more willing to releaſe others from it, that themſelves might be alſo free; and finding the People like well that they were ſo Indulged, they having laid aſide before, the Ends of Chriſt in Diſcipline, thought now how to ſerve Ends of their own; and thus diſpoſed, they ſoon found ways to ſerve both their Pride and Coveto uſneſs; ſetting up an undue Opinion of their Power in the Miniſtry, that their Miniſtry might be the more ſought to, and themſelves looked on as Perſons having full Power from God to Pardon Sinners; and abuſing the Rightful Authority thereof in Admitting Sinners to Reconciliation with the Church before their Penance; in enjoining alſo Penance afterwards to a different purpoſe than what it was intended firſt to ſerve, and with reſerve of Power to themſelves for making abatement thereof; by this means the Diſcipline of the Church was made a gain to them, but a loſs to Chriſtianity, became indeed
deſtructive

destructive to the Christian Religion and
the Souls of Sinners, instead of being as
in its design it was, and in its effect ought
to have been a Ministry promoting Godliness and the Salvation of Souls. For the
People, who are generally in love with
their Sins so far as to be well pleased when
they can find a means to reconcile the
hopes of Heaven with the enjoyment of
them, vainly thought it to be Peace,
which they obtained of the Church, not
solicitous, whether their Consciences were
purged from dead Works, or satisfaction
made to God for the appeasing his Wrath.
For this were they content to be deceived
of their Money by the Church, though
really to no effect, because seemingly they
had assurance given them by it of the Pardon of their Sins, and of exemption from
the Punishment of the same. This made
the Law of Auricular Confession superfti-
ously complyed with, it being a means
that giveth some colour for a man to per-
suade himself that he is reconciled to God,
though indeed it serve not the turn to
any manner of purpose, but is a cousen-
age that deludeth Souls to think that upon
the Priest's Absolution, the Score of their
Sins is cleared ; and that they may adven-
ture upon the same again at the hazard of
another Confession and giving content to
their Confessor.　　　　　　　　Now

' Now this great decay of Discipline, and vile corruption and abase of the Remains of it, in the last Ages, did loudly call for and necessarily require a Reformation in the Church; and the Reformation that hath been with us, hath well set aside the Abusers and put down the Corruptions that prevailed to the destruction of Christianity; but hath not re-established, or could not re-establish that Apostolical Discipline to the advantage of Christianity, which should have been restored in the Church of Christ when these were taken away. It is not hard to apprehend how it came to pass that the Church of *England* hath failed in that great piece of Reformation which it aimed at in this point, the receiving of publick Penance. Besides the common obstructions which all good Pretences will ever meet with, in all communities of Christians, from the Vices and Wickedness of men that always oppose the same; there might some particular Reasons be assigned in this case, why the desire of so evident a Reformation could not take place, when Reformation in the Church was so generally sought; from the share which Human Policy had in that Change which was brought to pass in the Church, and the different aim which many following that pursued, from what

those

thofe that had no other aim but the Reformation of the Church and the advantage of true Religion, endeavoured but could not to its full effect accomplish. But this Difcourfe is not fo much concerned in what might occafion this failure in our Reformation, as in this that the Church of *England* hath expreffed its aim at a Reformation in this Point, which it could not reach, and expreffed a Godly Defire, that in future time the *Primitive Difcipline* of the Church *may be reftored again.*

C H A P. VII.

AND now if by the Reafons and Arguments in this Tract offered to confideration, a Proof hath been made according to what I undertook for in the beginning, that is to fay, that Difcipline had place in the Primitive Church by the Ordinance of Chrift and his Apoftles; that Chrift left in his Church a Power and Authority for it, and the Apoftles gave in Charge for the Churches of their own Planting to be governed by it ; (which things I take to have been herein proved beyond contradiction, by Scripture interpreted according to the Senfe of the firft Chriftians;

tins, and so agreeably to Historical Truth,
that even common Sense justifieth the interpretation) It being also shewn what
Discipline the Apostles Instituted in the
Church; as also upon what ground and to
what purpose, by what the Church immediately after them did Practise; by what
was practised even throughout the whole
Church; (there being no part thereof but
what kept up a Discipline and agreed in
the necessity of doing so.) It likewise appearing to all that will see, that which is
plain to be seen in Church Writers of the
several Ages, by what degrees the Decay,
Abuses and Corruptions of Discipline
came on; that what now remaineth of it
as visibly deriveth it self from the Apostles, as the corrupt Christianity of this
time can derive it self from that which
they planted pure from the Fountain.
These things cannot but give conviction
that the Reformation of the Church consisteth in restoring of the Primitive Discipline to the use and effect it ought to have
in the Church of Christ. And that if our
first Reformers fell short of their Aim in
this Point, it is a work remaining for the
Church of the present Age to bring to
pass. And that an Obligation lieth on all
Ranks of Christians to do their parts towards it. As in the first place, on all that
                                      have

have share in the Office of the Ministry especially, forasmuch as Discipline is part of the Charge of their Ministry. Upon whom therefore as there is a necessity laid, that they *take heed to the Ministry, which they have received in the Lord, that they fulfill it,* I might in reason well suppose there should be less need, and yet as the case stands there is the more for my pressing the Obligation; in that though it cannot be thought that they do not see, or that they do not understand it, nevertheless it is apparent that they do little towards the discharge of it, but have suffered even those Remains of Discipline, which at the Reformation of our Church were with difficulty preserved, to lye neglected in such a manner that now they are even come almost to nothing. I take Grief therefore and even Shame to my self on this account, when I remind my Superiors and Brethren, helpers as my self in the Work of the Ministry, of what was

Vid. *Ordination of Bishops and Priests.*

professed to be our *Minds and Wills* in this particular, when *demand was made in the Name of God and of his Church* touching the same, of what was by us undertaken and promised at our admission to this Ministration in presence of the *Congregation of God's People,* whom we took to *bear witness* how we purposed and were *minded to* to behave our selves in the Church of God; and of the things given us in charge touching the same, when we received our Ministry in the Church : namely , that every Bishop in this our Church at the time he was admitted to that Administration, hath declared himself as to this Point, and promised faithfully that *by the help of God he would correct and punish the Disobedient and Criminous within his Diocess, according to such Authority as he hath by God's Word and as to him shall be committed by the Ordinance of this Realm* · hath likewise received it in Charge, to *be so Merciful that he be not too remiss, to minister Discipline, not forgetting Mercy ;* must also have fully known the intention of the Church as to what himself should do in this part of his Office, by that Prayer which it maketh to Almighty God , beseeching that he would *give Grace to all Bishops, the Pastors of his Church. that they may diligently preach his Word and duly administer the Godly Discipline thereof ;* as also by what was asked of God by the Church on behalf of himself in particular, that he would grant his Servant Grace *to use the Authority given him,* not to Destruction but to Salvation. That also every one admitted to the Order and Ministry of Priesthood within this Church hath undertaken and promised

P

that

that he will *by the help of the Lord,* give faithful diligence always so to Minister the Doctrine and Sacraments, and the *Discipline of Christ as the Lord hath commanded,* and as this Church and Realm hath received the same according to the Commandments of God ; as also that the *Lord being his helper* he will be ready with all faithful Diligence *to use both publick and private Monitions and Exhortations* as need shall require and occasion shall be given : And that as Power hath been committed to him by the imposition of hands for the office and work of a Priest in the Church of God, that Power which Christ gave for Discipline in his Church, *of retaining and remitting Sins* ; so he hath received a Charge with it to be a *faithful dispenser of the Word of God and of his holy Sacraments* ; which *faithful dispensation of the Sacraments* shall ever imply the discharge of that great Trust which God hath committed to them, to whom he hath given the Power of Ministring them, for the Ministration of the same according to the Terms of the Gospel, that none be allowed the assurance of their hopes as to God's Promises by these, but such as may reasonably be thought really and indeed qualified for those Promises which the Gospel tendreth. These things if we reflect on, and consider with our

selves

felves the nature and end of our Miniftry towards the Children of God, towards the Church of Chrift; we cannot want conviction that we ought, and in that refpect fhould not methinks want Perfuafion, never to ceafe our Labour and Diligence, until we have done all that lieth in us to reftore and bring to effect the Difcipline of Chrift's Church. Otherwife I cannot fee how it is poffible we fhould effectually and to the purpofe intended by Chrift difcharge the great Truft of our Miniftry ; as I fee not to what purpofe we pretend our felves to be Minifters of Chrift and of the Gofpel, in cafe we acknowledge not a Charge and Truft upon us to Minifter the Difcipline of Chrift as the Lord hath commanded. I do not fuppofe any Bifhop of the Church of *England* will pretend himfelf exonerated from the Charge laid upon him by Chrift and his Church, or from his own engagement thereupon, *to correct and punifh the Criminous according to fuch Authority as he hath by God's Word,* upon the account that 'tis required of him to do this according to *fuch Authority as fhall be committed to him by the Ordinance of this Realm :* Nor that any one called to the office of a Prieft in this Church will pretend to hold himfelf excufed from *Miniftring the Difcipline of Chrift*

as the Lord hath commanded, for that he is
alſo required to do this, *as this Church and
Realm hath received the ſame according to the
Commandments of God* : Which can never
be looked on as any Limitation upon the
Powers which the Church hath received
from Chriſt, but only as directing the'exerciſe thereof according to Form and Ceremony and Circumſtances. Or if any
ſhould go about to make uſe of this pretence, it will be to little purpoſe ; for
that the Diſcipline of Chriſt hath been
received, in ſome meaſure at leaſt, by this
Church and Realm, tho' not executed to
effect for the benefit of God's Church and
Intereſt of Chriſtianity, which is the fault
that cannot be accounted for. Moreover
both this Church and Realm have expreſly
taken notice of a failure in the deſigned
Reformation in this Point, ſo that it cannot be the deſign of the Laws or Ordinances of either to hinder or abridge the Diſcipline of Chriſt from being executed as
the Lord hath commanded. And beſides,
all ſuch as have received Orders in this
Church look upon themſelves, 'tis to be
hoped, as deputed to their Miniſtry *by Jeſus Chriſt,* though to be directed in thoſe
Functions which their Order importeth,
*by the Laws and Ordinances of this Church
and Realm :* And believe the effect of what
they

they do in all parts of their Office to be wrought *by the Power of Christ,* though their Office be exercised with effect *outwardly* by means of the *Laws of this Church and Realm* ; these affifting towards the doing the Work, but the Power of Christ producing the Spiritual end and purpofe of Converting the Soul. Confequently the Right, and Charge, and Truft appertaining to their refpective Offices muft be fuppofed to reft upon their Miniftries and to lye upon them as from Christ, that are incharged with the overfight and government of God's Church according to the Ordinance of Christ ; fo that by them fuch Miniftries muft be executed, were the Commonwealth not Christian ; and therefore even as it is Christian, much more they fhould be exercifed according to the Commandment of God and Christ : Infomuch that if our Church and Realm which pretend to have received the Difcipline of Christ according to the Commandment of God, and truly hath fo done fo far as the fame hath been received ; fhould indeed not have fo done, or fhould have received it to different purpofes, or fhould endeavour to fet it afide after it hath been received ; it will lye upon them who are Minifters of Christ and his Church, not of the State or Commonwealth ,

to acknowledge the Difcipline of Chrift
to Chriftian Purpofes, and ufe it to fuch
effect and not recede from their Power in
Chrift: Much more to endeavour to make
that Difcipline which the Ordinances of
the Church and Realm favour, effectual
to the Ends of Chrift and Intereft of Chriftianity; and likewife to let it be feen by
the effect of that Difcipline which is, how
much greater benefit it would be to Chriftian Religion to have it fully received according as by the Apoftles of Chrift it
was eftablished, and in the Primitive times
practifed in the Church of God; as well
as to infift upon the Right of the Church
to be allowed in the full Powers of its
Miniftry, being fuch as Chrift left with
his Church, and which are abfolutely
neceffary (which Chrift our Lord thought
fo or elfe he had not given them) for the
good Government of his Church. This
therefore I fhall leave with the Confcience
of all that are admitted to the Miniftry in
the Church, after I have faid this one
word, that this is an Office of the Miniftry exprefly given in Charge by the Holy
Scriptures, and is in its nature as effectual
through the Power of Chrift to faving
Purpofes as any other Charge of our Miniftry whatfoever; even the Difpenfation
of the Sacraments is not a more neceffary

part of the Ministry, yea this is implied in the faithful Dispensation of these. For not to speak of what is by the Corruption of men, but what ought to be by the appointment of God, it is a thing undeniable, That the Right of Communicating with the Church in the Holy Sacrament, is not to be allowed any by the Ministry of the Church, but upon such Terms and according to such Rules, that a Man being qualified according to them, may be also qualified for those Promises which the Gospel tendreth; which the Discipline of the Church, *i. e.* they that have the Ministry of its Discipline are to see to and bring to pass.

These things also make it the Common Concern of all Christians to have the Discipline of Christ Received and Established in the Church for the good of Souls. For so long as the Church is without Discipline, the Members thereof must be without the benefit thereof to their Souls; and how to supply that want to themselves, is probably not known to the greatest part; and 'tis questionable as to more, whether they will be so true to the Interest of their Souls, as to supply of their own accord, that which is lacking in the Church's Ministry. Now that Defect which is in the Ministry in this Case, must remain, unless

the

the Members of the Church confent to allow the Miniftry in its full Powers, and fubmit to the Authority thereof; for that our Lord Chrift hath not indued the Minifters of his Kingdom with any outward or Temporal Power to conftrain Obedience, neither in this, nor any other Cafe. The Laws of Kingdoms and Commonwealths may indeed fomething inforce the Execution and outward Effect of this Miniftry; but the inward End is wrought by the Spiritual Power which the Conscience of a Chriftian acknowledgeth. Hence all Chriftians become concerned to receive, and acknowledge the Spiritual Inftitutions of the Gofpel and the Power of the fame to the purpofes of God and Chrift; Having reafon to believe, that Chrift will give them Power and Efficacy to attain their Ends when Adminiftred in his Name, and according to his Will, and that becaufe they are *His*; (if fo be they are received as his Inftitutions by them that are obliged fo to receive them, and to be fubject unto them); and having caufe to receive them as fuch, their Inftitution appearing in the Scriptures, together with Powers given for bringing them to Effect, and Rules prefcribed therein for making them moft ferviceable to Chriftian Ends. This is the thing that maketh it to lie upon all Chriftians

ftians to receive the Word of God Preached, not as the Word of Men, but (as it is in Truth) the Word of God, which will effe-ctually work in them when they believe: And this accordingly maketh it neceffary that the Difcipline of the Church be ac-knowledged to be the Difcipline of Chrift, and, that the Power of Chrift be believed to render it effectual to faving purpofes towards them, that out of Confcience fub-mit thereto.

But in as much as Men are Chriftians now more upon Motives of Intreft than Confcience, as in that refpect it is to be feared they may not be willing to fubmit themfelves to the Difcipline of Chrift or his Church, their Love they have to their Sins having made them Refolute and Head-ftrong, Impatient of Reproof, Correction, or Cenfure in their Unchriftian way of liv-ing ; fo that tho' it might be hoped of the better part, they would be enclinable out of Confcience, to fubmit to the Church in this its Miniftry ; neverthelefs it can-not be thought of the greater part, that they will do it of their voluntary Will: This maketh it neceffary that the State, being Chriftian, fhould lend its Affiftance to the Miniftry of the Church, to Com-pafs and Effect the Eftablifhment of the Primitive Difcipline. For, how is the
State

State Chriftian, but as it maintaineth the Minifters of Chrift's Church in doing their Office, and enforceth the effect of their Miniftry upon thofe that would not otherwife be Subject, or yield Obedience to them? It muft be allowed, I grant, to every State, to judge of that wherein the Church defireth Affiftance from it, whether it be part of that Chriftianity which it hath undertaken to maintain, as alfo, what Courfe is to be taken therein agreeable to the tenour of Scripture, if poffible, in the firft place, and yet, fuch as may agree alfo with the Neceffities of the Kingdom in which the Church findeth its Protection. For even all Private Chriftians are allowed the Judgment of particular Difcretion to difcharge unto God, even in Matters of Religion, the account of what themfelves do: therefore is this Judgment rather to be allowed to Perfons in Publick Authority, to confider in what they are to lend, or refufe their Affiftance to the Minifters of the Church in their Office, under the account they are to give to God as they are Chriftians, and as they are Sovereign Powers; in the latter of which Capacities they muft be allowed to have Confideration of the Neceffities of the Kingdom under their Civil Government. Not that they may, for what by them fhall be judged

the

the neceſſities of the Kingdom, put down,
or obſtruct the Church in any part of the
Miniſtry which ſhe hath Right to Execute
with Powers from Chriſt, which muſt always be left to their full Effect upon the
Conſciences of Men, or elſe the State Ty-
rannizeth over, and Perſecuteth the
Church; but that they may refuſe to enforce the Miniſtry of the Church with
other External Power; and Force than the
Neceſſities of the State will allow; yet
this ſtill under the account they muſt give
to God for the Protection of Chriſtianity, which as Chriſtians they are obliged
to, in the beſt manner that they can judge
their Secular Power may be employed
for that purpoſe. Having ſaid this, it is
not my deſign, any one may be ſure, to
inſiſt, that the Sovereign Power, being
Chriſtian, is under an abſolute Obligation
to enforce the Cenſures of the Church with
Temporal Coercions and Penalties. For I
take it to be but conjecture at moſt, which
hath been urged in this Caſe by ſome,
That God impowred the Apoſtles to enforce their Cenſures with Bodily Puniſh-
ments upon Offenders, for that the Church
was deſtitute of the Protection of Secular
Powers to conſtrain by outward Force,
ſubmiſſion to its Authority; and that a-
gainſt the time that this extraordinary
Power

Power should cease, he provided the Protection of Secular Powers for the Maintainance of Christianity; that this therefore should oblige these Powers to enforce the determination and Censures of the Church in all Cases with Temporal Penalties, to make the same be always received, and submitted to. For though it be true, that the Apostles had such an extraordinary Power from God, in respect of which, the Censure, which put Offenders out of the Church is called a delivering to Satan, because, by some Plague on the Body, it appeared that they came within his Power so soon as put out of the Church; yet there appeareth another reason for this, namely, that it might be a confirmation of God's Power in, and with the Ministry of his Church, which ceased when God saw fit, and that sufficient Confirmation had been given of the Presence and Power of God with his Church and with the Ministry thereof: And besides, it is pretended without Proof, that this extraordinary Effect followed the Censures of the Church all the time that the Church wanted the Assistance of the Civil Magistrate; and if it were true, it would not be sufficient to infer the Consequence, that this should oblige Secular Powers to confirm the Censures of the
Church

Church always against Stubborn Sinners with standing Penalties. Nevertheless; if the Civil Power, which being Christian, ought to Cherish the Church in its Bosom, will Protect the Church in its Ministry; it must in this Case not abridge the Church's Ministry, nor lay any Restraint upon her Powers, but allow the Ministers thereof according to their Office to Govern the Church by the Discipline of Christ. It must so far Protect and Maintain the Church in this its Ministry, as to restrain any that may go about to disturb the Peace of the Church in respect of her Censures. It ought to re-estate the Church and its Synods in their full Right, if they have been outed of such Right, or otherwise to own and acknowledge the Right of the Church, to prescribe Rules, and make necessary Laws for restoring the Publick Discipline of Penance in the Church, being an Ordinance of our Lord and his Apostles, Abolished indeed by Injury of Time, and Corruption in the Manners and Principles of Christians, but necessary to be restored in respect of the Obligation upon the Church to Execute the Ministry of Christ in all its parts; as well as in respect of the Evils and Mischief to Christianity that have been found to proceed from the want thereof. It ought to procure, sure, that Men set a due esteem upon the Communion of the Church, and that they fear the Sentence of Excommunication, if not for Temporal Penalties which Civil Laws may make consequent thereon; however at least, by so far Privileging those that hold and seek Communion with the Church, as that no Man may find his Interest in standing out against the Church, and despising her Censures. I take it for granted, that if a State will Protect the Church, it cannot do less than this; it must allow it the Exercise of its Ministry, or it doth not allow it to be a Church; and as it cannot be said to allow its Ministry unless the whole be allowed, so it can never be supposed to be in the Power of a State to lay a Restraint upon any part thereof, but for the same Reason that this shall be judged Lawful, it shall be Lawful for a State to set aside the whole Ordinance of our Lord and his Apostles. It must preserve and keep the Church from Violence and Force, whilst it proceedeth according to its own Rules; or otherwise, the Church, as a Church hath not Protection. It must not wrest any Powers from the Church, nor take them to it self, for that destroyeth the Society of the Church, that this is no more a Society; being without the necessary Powers of a Society, enabling

enabling it to act for the ends and purposes of its Constitution. The State must
likewise own and acknowledge the Right of
the Church to prescribe and make Rules
that shall have the Authority of Laws
within the Church, for bringing to Effect
the Ministry and Ordinances of our Lord
and his Apostles; otherwise the State taketh upon it to set aside, or make void
the Trust and Power which Christ hath
left and committed to his Church. And
for that I take it, there are but Two Reasons, in respect of which the Church can
be said to be Protected by the State, that
is to say, in respect either of Privileges
to such as hold Communion with the
Church, or Penalties on such as do not;
I, (who have not insisted that Secular
Powers are bound to Protect the Church
by inflicting Penalties upon all those that
are not of it, but that they may act therein as to themselves shall seem meet, having regard to the Constitution and Necef-
sities of their State, and to another thing
not as yet mentioned, namely, that there
can be no constraint to true Christianity
by Temporal Punishment, that therefore
it is by no means reasonable in this Case to
make use of the utmost Penalties) must
yet insist, that where the Church hath Protection, there be such Privileges to those
that

that hold Communion with it, as that Men following the Reason of Privilege and of Christianity together, may set an esteem upon the Communion of the Church, and fearing the loss of Temporal Privileges upon being excluded from the Communion of the Church, may be induced to submit to the Church, and what course of Penance that may prescribe to prevent the loss of their Souls. It will be said (for it is said already as to what the Civil Power hath with us done for the Protection and Advancement of Christianity, that this may make Hypocrites, but not True Christians) this may cause some Persons to hold Communion with the Church, and to submit to Terms for sake of Privileges which Communion with the Church affordeth, more than for the sake of Christianity, or any inward esteem that they have of the Church's Communion, and the Spiritual Advantages that affordeth. And truly, 'tis not unlikely that Hypocritical Profession may many times follow that which Secular Powers do at any time with purpose of advancing Christianity, or giving Countenance or Authority to the Church of Christ: But 'tis more than probable also, that the Assistance which the State may give to the Church may be to good purpose, as Men being kept by

Laws

Laws of their Country to hold Communion with the Church, and for that to avoid such Scandalous Practices as must otherwise exclude them that Communion, to their-Prejudice, may be won in time by seeing the Effect of Christianity and the Ministry thereof, to the Reformation of Mens Lives among whom they live, to allow the same to have effect also upon their own Hearts and Lives. It is upon this latter probability that Christian States have always Acted, when they have given Assistance to Religion, or the Church; and the probability on this side will ever be of weight, 'tis to be hoped, with Christian Powers, to Act with a good meaning and purpose for the Interest of Christianity under the Account they are to give to God; for employing the Authority he has given them in the World, to his Service and Honour; so as the possibility on the other side, that the Wickedness of Men may defeat their good purpose, and the best measures they can take shall not however hinder them from doing what on their part may be done, and what it is their Duty to do, as they profess Christianity, and the Maintainance of God's Church.

I may not however after all this, pretend to say, what the Supreme Power of this Kingdom ought to do for the Esta-

Q blish

ment of the Church's Discipline. What
it may do, and what it is reasonable it
should, are things to be considered by Su-
periours in the Church, when these shall
take into Consideration how the Discipline
of Christ's Church may be Restored, and
may then be fit to be represented to the
Authority of the Kingdom. Only indeed,
if the Church be under such Restraint of
Temporal Laws, that her Synods cannot
enter into Consultation, how to bring
the Ordinances of Christ and his Apostles into Effect ; the State will be Answe-
rable to God for the Obstruction to the
Ordinance and Ministry of Christ, if such
Restraint be not taken off ; that the Ecclesiastical Synods of this Church may be left
free to Consult and Act for the Maintenance of our Common Christianity, and
of the Church that Ministreth thereto,
and particularly in this very Case, how
by wholesom Discipline to restrain those
Vices and Enormities, which at present De-
face our Church, and have Sullied all
her Glory, have Corrupted Religion, and
Debauched Men's Lives and Principles to a
great degree. When *Men's Sins are thus*
open before-hand, going before to Judgment,
openly calling for the Censures and Judgment of the Church, to put a Restraint upon such Practices, there ought to be the
                                    strictest

ftricteft Difcipline, and in fuch Circumftances our Ecclefiaftical Synod ought to
call to mind the Work of the firft Councils and Synods in the Church, to give
Effect to that Difcipline which Chrift left
inherent in his Church for the Support
and Maintenance of Chriftianity, fo as to
act after their Example. And in fhort,
fuch is the neceffity of a Reformation, that
thofe that bear the Power of the Church
can never be Excufable in a farther neglect
of their Duty in this Cafe; and the Authority of the Kingdom will be alfo chargeable with much of the Guilt, if pretending to act with Authority in the Church
after the Example of the Pious Kings of
God's People, who employed their Authority to reduce the Law into Practice, it
oblige not thofe who have the Power of
the Church trufted with them, to give
Effect to the Ordinance of our Lord and
his Apoftles in this particular; and concur
not with them thereunto.

C H A P.   VIII.

I Muft not pafs over in this place the
confideration of feveral Pretences that
are commonly offered in excufe for our
having

having laid aſide the Diſcipline of Chriſt's
Church, or at leaſt, for our not endeavouring to retrieve and reſtore it.

Now againſt the Reſtoring of Diſcipline, ſome ſay, that it is ſufficient for
the Edification of the Church, that the
Goſpel ſhould be *Preached in it,* ſince that
is the Ordinary means which God has appointed to procure the Converſion and
the Salvation of Men. If this Pretence
had any thing of Reaſon in it, I might nevertheleſs argue for the neceſſity of Diſcipline in the preſent Circumſtances of the
Church, upon the account that the Ordinance of Preaching is not now of that
Efficacy as it was in the times of the Apoſtles, that then there were Extraordinary
Graces and Powers accompanied the
Preaching of the Word, that gave it an
influence and efficacy greatly beyond any
Effects thereof that are at preſent ſeen,
or may be now expected. So that there
is a great miſtake in the commonly received Opinion of the efficacy of the *Word
Preached.* But this I need not inſiſt on;
for, allowing to the Ordinance of Preaching as great efficacy now as it had in the
firſt beginnings of the Goſpel, nevertheleſs it is but one among other means of
God's appointment for to bring to paſs the
Converſion and Salvation of Men, there
are

are besides this, the Sacraments and Discipline prescribed in, and by the Gospel of Christ. Now all the Ordinances being instituted by the same Power, it is even most necessary for the Reputation of the Wise Contrivance of them, that no one Ordinance should supersede the use of the other, but in respect of the Divine Institution there is an Obligation to keep up the respect and use of every Ordinance, it not being to be supposed that the Divine Wisdom would have appointed any but what must be of use and benefit, which benefit will be lost, if there be not an use of the Ordinance. This is the case, as to *Preaching the Word,* it was, and is, an effectual means for the Conversion of Men to Christianity ; and a Grace goeth with it for that purpose ; but after Men are wrought to Believe, and Profess Christianity, they are concerned to live suitably to that Profession : Now though by the present use of Preaching Men may be Convinced of the necessity of a Holy Life, yea, suppose them brought to the greatest and most serious sense of this Necessity ; yet they stand in need of farther Grace, to enable them to practise Holiness ; this makes the use of the Sacraments necessary, from which that assistance may be expected ; and must it not reasonably be

Q 3   thought

thought that they stand in need also of that care which the Church taketh to keep them to the strict performance of their Christian Duty, when as our Lord Christ hath appointed Government and a Discipline in his Church for that purpose, having set, and appointed the Ministers of his Church to watch over his Flock that they go not astray? Can any Man assure himself that his own heart shall at no time deceive him, so as that he may need and receive benefit in the concerns of his Soul, from the watch and care which Christ hath required the Faithful Pastors of his Church to keep and take, in reference to the Souls committed to their Charge? 'Tis certain the Pastors of Christ's Church cannot but know the chief part of their Function to be the Conduct and Government of the Church, and that though now-a-days the whole Ministry seems placed in the business of Sermons; there is another Trust upon them for the Conduct and Government of the Church, and this they know to be a Charge of the greatest moment; therefore why they should suppose they are not to account to God for this as well as any other Office of their Ministry I cannot see. Whoever looks into what S. *Paul* hath writ, concerning the Duties of the Ministry, and shall examine

amine what he says of that Charge and of the Qualifications of those who are to be admitted into it, will find that he insists upon the Government of the Church as the Principal Charge of the Ministry; as hath been shewn already out of the Epistles to *Timothy* and *Titus.* It must be therefore said, that those who think Preaching can answer all the occasions of the Church, are wiser than Christ and his Apostles; but those Pastors, who can be content that the Discipline of Christ's Church be laid aside to please the Humour of those who are content to hear what Ecclesiasticks have to say for the Christian Religion, but resolved to live as please themselves; will be chargeable before God for that Corruption of the People, which is the consequence of the Loss of the Church's Discipline, and for betraying the greatest Trust of their Ministry so far as they have consented to lay this Discipline aside.

But others perhaps will say, that Discipline is not essential to Religion; it is a matter of Order only, and therefore as it cannot be of very great Moment, so there may be Liberty to use or not use it, as the Church shall see occasion. To this I answer: That it is true there are in Christianity, Things immediately necessary

to

to the Salvation of Particular Christians, relating to Faith or good Manners ; and there are other Things necessary to the publick Order and Government of the Church, that by it Christians, may be edified in all matters of the first kind. The Things of the first kind are indeed of the greatest Moment as immediately concerning the Salvation of Christians, yet those of the latter kind are of Importance and Necessity in the Church, as the Church is constituted a Society and the Ministry thereof appointed for the Assisting and Edifying Christians in the things of their Salvation. It is not pretended that there is not Salvation to be had for Christians without Discipline, nor that there are not means of Salvation in a Church where Discipline is not ; for some may have that probity of Heart as may resolve them to become good Christians of themselves, whether the Church take any care of them or not ; and more may be wrought by the word Preached to a serious Sense of the necessity of a Holy Life ; and though left to themselves to look to the qualifying of themselves for the Sacraments of Christ's Church, whereby they receive the Divine Grace to enable them to live that Life, may out of a true concern for their Souls take a faithful care to come to the Sacraments

ments fo Qualified as God requires, and
may by that means obtain Grace and work
out their Salvation. But inafmuch as more
might be brought ftill to live the Life of
Chriftians were the full Miniftry of the
Church imployed for this purpofe, and
more Benefit would accrue to the greater
part of Chriftians by the Church's looking after, and feeing them qualified duely
for the Sacraments according to what is
required in the Gofpel for Benefit to be
had thereby ; in this refpect it muft be faid
that there are not all the means of Salvation in a Church, where Difcipline is not ;
and that no Church can be at Liberty to
ufe or not ufe this which is a Neceffary
part of its Miniftry as being of Chrift's
Inftitution, and is one of thofe means of
Salvation which the Church is intrufted
to furnifh and fupply to Chriftians, who
are to be kept and conducted by the Miniftry thereof in the way to Salvation.
It is not to be pretended that this is a
weak means and therefore the lefs to be
regarded. For as to the Spiritual Inftitutions of the Gofpel, How are any capable of judging, which are Weaker which
Stronger, when as they come all to effect
by the Invifible Power of God ? For this
reafon they are to be thought always fufficient for the accomplifhment of the Ends,
where-

whereunto they are defigned, as they have a Powerful though fecret Influence on the Confciences of men : being his Inftitutions who is Lord of their Confciences, and who knoweth how to give them Power and Efficacy to attain their Ends, and will do it becaufe they are His Ordinances. And therefore the Difcipline of Chrift's Church being a Spiritual Ordinance, that conducteth and keepeth within the bounds of Chriftian Religion the Profeffors thereof; by a conftraining Force indeed, but this not fuch as affecteth either Men's Bodies or their Eftates, but fuch as is a Spiritual Force that is efficacious and operating upon the Heart and Confciences of Men, is not to be thought a weak means or flight part of the Miniftry of God's Church, fo as on that account to be flighted by thofe that are to bring the Miniftry of the Church to effect for the faving of Souls. But on the contrary 'tis rather to be confidered, by them that have the Truft of this Miniftry, that St. *Paul* hath faid concerning it, that the *Weapons thereof are not carnal but mighty through God,* and that the ufe of his *Power which the Lord hath given him* in this cafe would be a *proof of Chrift's being with* him, who was not *weak* but *mighty :* That therefore this Miniftry of the Church, were it, as in former

mer

2 Cor. 10. 4.

mer days, in some measure acted rightly
and zealously towards the known ends
of it, such as by all it must be acknowledged useful and neceffary to, if there be
a force and efficacy in it : the fame will
still have its Effect upon all truly confcientious as in the Primitive Church ; and
this might make more to be confcientious,
and God by the Power of his Spirit invi-
fibly affifting (as there is reason to believe he is pleafed to affift all his own Ordinances when his Church faithfully Ad-
miniftreth the fame according to His Mind
and Will, and for the ends of his Glory, or
ends by Him appointed) might be a means
to restore the now well-nigh loft Government of the Church and Practice of Religion.

But 'tis likely that it will be said, That
the Zeal of the Primitive Chriftians is ex-
tinct, that Men are now very Corrupt and
not to be brought to a fubmiffion to the
Difcipline of the Church, yea the generality are of a Temper that will make that
Difcipline not liked even by good Men,
But this very thing that Men are Corrupt
is an argument for the neceffity of Difcipline. This Reafon maketh Difcipline
more neceffary now than it was in the firft
Ages of the Church, when the Chriftian
Church was not fo Corrupt, when Perfecution

cution kept Corruption out of the Church: When the Church is in Peace Vices and Scandals multiply, and then is good Discipline moſt neceſſary. It muſt be owned indeed, that as the ſtate of Diſeaſed Bodies ſometimes will not admit of the proper Remedies, ſo the Corruption of Chriſtians is grown to that heighth as that it will hardly be brought to admit the proper method of Cure. But as the skilful Phyſitian does not give over the Diſeaſe for deſperate in every weak Conſtitution, but ſeeks to help the Infirmities of a weak Body, that it may be able to bear the application of proper Remedies : So ſhould every Phyſitian of Souls encounter the Prejudices, which (in our corrupt State and lewd Age, not bearing ſtrict reſtraint or controul) men may have againſt the Diſcipline of Chriſt's Church ; and for this purpoſe carefully inſtruct the People concerning the neceſſity of Diſcipline, preparing them as they may for it, ſhewing their Prejudices againſt it to be unreaſonable, ariſing chiefly from Luſts, that if ſuffered to prevail, will deſtroy their Souls ; and convincing them that the Diſcipline of Chriſt's Church is the wholeſome neceſſary Phyſick to cure the great Corruption of the preſent time. Endeavours being uſed to this purpoſe, there is good ground to be-

believe a poſſibility of ſucceſs; for if it was a thing impoſſible to bring men under the Diſcipline of Chriſt, God would never have appointed it in his Church. The wickedneſs of Men at all times obſtructeth the means of God's appointment for bringing men off from ſuch Wickedneſs, and the greater this groweth the more is the obſtruction at all times; if therefore Vice and Licentiouſneſs be ſtrong and prevalent, as now, the Church and her Miniſters that are concerned to oppoſe and give ſtop to its progreſs, are in that reſpect the more concerned not to recede from, or part with any Part or Powers of their Miniſtry, but rather to make full Proof thereof to the utmoſt effect poſſible in the caſe; only taking heed to this, the management of the Powers of their Miniſtry with neceſſary Prudence, which may render the exerciſe of the ſame effectual, according to what Circumſtances the Church may be in, or what Temper thoſe particular men may be of with whom they have to do, or what may be the Diſcipline of the generality of Chriſtians: All which may deſerve regard in the management of the Powers of our Miniſtry; though there ought not regard to be had to any or all of them for the laying aſide any Part of that Miniſtry by which the Church

of

of Chrift is to be governed according to his appointment. It muft be owned, 'tis true, as to the prefent Temper of the generality of Chriftians, it is fuch, as probably would render the Difcipline of Chrift's Church uneafy to the moft confcientious Chriftians, if they were to pafs through it; in refpect of the Shame and Ignominy which the Lewdnefs of vulgar Chriftians might be apt to expofe thofe to, who out of Chriftian Simplicity, and true Humility, and inward Sorrow of Heart for their Sins might be content to receive Penance from the Church. This is an Evil, but fuch as may be removed by fhewing men the evil and mifchief of fuch Lewdnefs as fhall work and infult over, not only the failings and infirmities of their Chriftian Brethren but alfo their Devotion and Humility; their Sorrow and Contrition of Heart, and even turn the folemn Ordinance of Chrift into Ridicule. It muft be fhewn that St. *Paul* hath given a Rule to all Chriftians in this cafe, that if

Gal. 6. 1, *a man be overtaken in a fault, thofe which*
2. *are Spiritual, fhould reftore fuch a one in the Spirit of meeknefs, confidering themfelves left they alfo be tempted,* and that he requireth of Chriftians to *bear one anothers burthens and fo fulfil the Law of Chrift :* that is to fay, that in cafes of this nature, men fhould

should at all times confider, how poffible it is, that they themfelves may fall into the like Sin in time of Temptation, and in that regard fhould by no means infult over their Brethren overtaken in a Fault, but rather pity them and be concerned for them, having forrow on their behalf, feeking to recover them out of the fnare of the wicked one ; and praying for them, that it would pleafe God to give them Repentance unto Life. Men muft be put in mind of the Primitive Chriftians who Sympathifed with their Brethren in fuch a manner, that the whole Affembly did Mourn and Lament when the Cenfures of the Church paft on Sinners, or when fuch were admitted to Penance ; bewailing in the former cafe the circumftances and fad ftate of the Sinner, and in the latter cafe Solicitous for their Reconcilement with God. It muft be fhewn that Chriftian Charity *rejoyceth not in iniquity, but rejoyceth in the Truth,* i. e. it truly rejoyceth to fee men difcharge their Chriftian Duty and live in all manner of *fincerity* ; but it rejoyceth not, it is fad and extremly grieved at all Wickednefs, it maketh a Man truly grieve and mourn at any Sin committed by any other, much more at the mifcarriages of a Chriftian Brother ; for whom as a Chriftian hath a more near concern, fo he ought

1 Cor 13. 6.

to have the greater compaſſion, when he
ſeeth him Offend to the hazard of his Soul,
and to the diſhonour and reproach of the
Chriſtian Name. and Profeſſion. 'Tis to
be ſuppoſed that a careful repreſentation
of theſe things might bring the generality
of Chriſtians to ſuch a Temper of Charity and Meekneſs and Purity, as that they
neither would triumph nor inſult over the
failures and infirmities of their Chriſtian
Brethren ; nor make ſport with their Penitence and Devotion ; nor take Pleaſure
to themſelves and mock at ſuch Wicked-
neſſes as may come under Publick Reproof or Cenſure ; which is a thing that
betrays a ſecret Love to Wickedneſs in
thoſe that are ſo vile as to make a ſport
thereof, and giveth occaſion to good men
of diſlike to the Diſcipline of the Church,
when as their Submiſſion to it expoſeth
them to contempt and ſhame with diſſo-
lute Chriſtians. Nevertheleſs if this
Lewdneſs may not be preſently nor álto-
gether taken away and removed, thoſe
Chriſtians who may ſtand in need of being
inſtructed by the Church to Repentance,
muſt be informed and perſuaded that they
conſult very ill for themſelves, if they are
more mindful of their Shame than of their
Salvation ; that being conſcious to themſelves of their Sins, they have reaſon to
take

take Shame to themselves in that respect; and though indeed it no way becomes their Fellow Christians to make them a contempt and scorn, yet especially, as themselves have deserved worse at the hands of God, that shame which in respect of themselves and their Sins is just, though no other than unreasonable and sinful folly in those that reproach them with it, should not hinder them from submitting to that course of Penance prescribed by the Church's Discipline as necessary to prevent the future Punishment of their Sins and save their Souls. It is to be considered moreover by them that are to bring the Discipline of the Church to effect, that this Lewdness began to spring early in the Church: There were in *Origen*'s time those that did upbraid, mock and deride their Christian Brethren upon the account of things which were confessed in Penance. *Tertullian* indeed argues that no good Christian could be guilty of such wicked Folly; and he said right, for it is a contradiction to the Law of Christian Charity, and the Spirit of Humility and Meekness; but yet even in his time there were some Professors of Christianity that committed this Folly; and he found this mischief from it, that many shunned the work of Penance upon it, being *more mindful of their*

Shame, as he fays, *than of their Salvation.* But he was far from allowing this to be an Excufe for thofe that drew back from the Difcipline of the Church on this account, or that the Church might wave its Difcipline for this reafon. It is true, that feems to have given occafion for the Church's fubftituting afterwards Private Confeffion inftead of Publick; but this at firft was only of fecret Faults voluntarily Confeffed, by that means to draw more to feek of themfelves the affiftance of the Church in their Repentance for their Secret Sins, when thefe were not to be publifhed to the Ears of the People, but only to be laid open to the Penitentiary that was appointed to take their Confeffion and inftruct them in Repentance. Still the Difcipline of the Church brought open Sins to Publick Confeffion; and from the time that firft this came to be abated, thence may be dated the Decay and Abufe of Difcipline. To pretend therefore the diffolute Behaviour of Chriftians to be a Reafon that will juftify the not reftoring the Difcipline of the Church, is but in a manner the fame thing as to fay, There is no Blame nor Fault in this that it hath been fuffered to Decay and fall to Nothing. Which yet I do not fuppofe any Chriftian will plainly fay or avouch.

It

It will be said probably, that the want of Discipline in the Church is supplied by the Authority of the Civil Magistrate, as in all places where the Civil Power is Christian, and the Authority thereof employed to suppress Vice and Licentiousness. It must be acknowledged indeed, that the Power of the Civil Magistrate is of God's Appointment, to be a Terror to them that do Evil, and that Civil Punishments are of great use, to restrain and suppress Vice and Wickedness at all times. But nevertheless, this cannot be a Reason for the Discipline of the Church to be laid aside, which is of Christ's Institution. The one is of use, but the other is much more useful to the effect of Reformation. The Magistrates Power reacheth only to the outward Behaviour, but the Discipline of the Church hath Effect on the Heart and Conscience ; neither the one nor the other, its true, can take hold of any but open and known Sins, but the Operation of the latter extendeth to work the heart to Contrition for the same, and to an inward Resolution of Amendment, whereas the Civil Power restraineth only the outward Act. It must be owned indeed farther, that even the Discipline of the Church, (considering the present disposition of Men in this Corrupt

State of Christianity) is of more Force, when it is supported by the Authority of Civil Powers. Nevertheless, the Civil Authority must not for this supersede the use of Ecclesiastical Discipline, nor be thought sufficient to Reclaim Sinners, and Reform the Church of Christ. The Discipline of the Church and that of the Magistrate are distinct Things; the one has its effect upon the Conscience by the Power of Christ, though it may come to some effect outwardly also by the help of that other, whose Power is from outward Force and Punishment. Both these therefore have their use, and should accordingly be employed to effect a Reformation. I allow therefore the Zeal of many that have made an Attempt lately in this Kingdom towards a Reformation of Manners, by putting in Execution the Penal Laws against Wickedness and Prophaness, to be good and commendable; but the Corruption and Lewdness of the Age requires a more effectual Remedy, that is to say, the Restoring of the Church Discipline. There hath been lately Publish'd *Account of* an Account of several Societies formed in *the Societies* this Kingdom to Effect a Reformation of *for Refor-* Manners, by putting in Execution the Laws *mation,&c.* of the Realm against Prophaness and Debauchery. The Design seems to be very good,

good, but the Method wrong, for that the forming of Societies for Reformation of Manners out of thofe that are already Members of a Chriftian Church, feems to carry with it a Reproach to the Society of the Church, Conftituted it felf for that purpofe. And the Argument of that Author, That *Chriftians of all Ranks* are obliged in Confcience to engage in Societies for the purpofe of having the Laws of the Kingdom put in Execution againft Prophanefs, as the moft proper means to compafs a National Reformation, and moft likely to prove for that end effectual, doth feem to imply, either that the Church whereof they are Members is not a Society for fuch purpofe, or that this Society hath not proper Means and Power of its own to bring it to pafs. For the Church being a Society Conftituted for the purpofe of our being kept therein to live Chriftian and Holy Lives, and all Chriftians bound to become Members of the Church, and fubject to thofe that Govern in it; the forming of another Society within the Church feemingly reflecteth on the reft of our Chriftian Brethren, and on the Church it felf whereof all are Members. And if the Church be a Society with Powers from Chrift to oblige itsMembers to live Chriftianly, it muft be the firft Concern of Chrifti-

ans

ans to allow those Powers their Force, and bring to effect for this purpose the Discipline of the Church. Not but that the Authority of the Kingdom hath done well in making Laws for punishing Wickedness, and there lieth also an Obligation according to the Stations and Offices Men may be in, and bear within the Kingdom, to put these Laws in Execution, and their doing it is Service to God as well as to their Country. Yet the Obligation lying upon all as Christians, and upon the Clergy especially, that bear the Power of the Church, is of another nature, that is to say, it lieth upon all as Christians to restore one another in the way of Charity, to seek the Recovery of a Brother from the Snare of the Devil, and the saving of his Soul by the Methods that Christianity directeth, i. e. fraternal Correpton, Admonition, Exhortation, Reproof, &c. and upon the Clergy to endeavour this by doing their diligence in their Function, by acting according to the Powers of their Ministry in all things, and bringing to effect the Discipline of Christ. And therefore setting aside the particular Obligation upon Kings, Governors, and Magistrates, and Subordinate Officers of the Kingdom to see to the due Execution of the Laws thereof; I see nothing in Christianity that

that makes it the *Common Duty of all Men*
(as the Author of the *Account* would have it)
to give Informations to the Magistrate one
against another, that all Wickedness may be
punished with Temporal Penalties, nor
that it is the *Particular Province* of those
who have entred into the Places of *Overseers* and *Watch-men*, that is, of the Ministers of Christ's Church, to *teach all Men
that this is their Duty* as Christians, nor
that it should lie upon them in any respect to promote themselves Informations
of this kind before the Civil Powers.
There is a sad Truth indeed insisted on
by that Authr in more places than one of
his Book, to wit, *That there is little or no
Reason to expect Help or Redress against the
Wickedness of the Age from the Ecclesiastical
Power by telling Offences to the Church, the
Ecclesiastical Power being weakned, and the
Discipline of the Church, which if it had been
in Force, might have proved a Bank against
the Flood of Wickedness that is broken in upon us, being now so lost, that it is of little use
for the purpose of Reformation.* But is this
come to pass through the fault only of them
that bear the Power of the Church, and
through their neglect only that the Discipline of the Church is of no effect? If so,
it is fit the Authority of the Kingdom
should oblige 'em to Act according to their

R 4   Duty,

Duty, and according to the Charge and Power of their Miniftry. But if it be, that a feveral Corruption is the Occafion of this, it will lie upon all Chriftians to fupport in all they can the Difcipline of the Church againft the prevailing Power of Wickednefs. If it be, that thofe who ought to exercife Difcipline for the giving a ftop to wickednefs, have not now the power to do it, as being under Limitations in the Exercife of their Miniftry; it muft lie upon the Authority of the Kingdom, to fee that reftraint taken off, and to reftore the Church to its Right and Power for the Miniftring of Difcipline. In the mean time there is, I grant, the greater Reafon for the Authority of the Kingdom to employ its Power to fupprefs Vice, to ftop the Avenues to Wickednefs, and take out of publick view the Contagion of bad Example. It doth alfo the more concern Private Chriftians to labour every one with his Brother the Promotion of Piety and Godlinefs, by Exhortation, Admonition, Reproof and good Example, and all other Charitable and Chriftian Methods for this End. There is the greater Reafon for the Clergy alfo to labour with diligence in the other works of their Miniftry. But why this fhould be a Reafon for thofe to go beyond their Miniftry I do not fee. By this

this Method to Prepare Men the better for the *Reftoration of Godly Difcipline* (fays that Author); But probably there is caufe to think, that Attempts of this kind by the Clergy might rather obftruct the Reftoration of that Difcipline, and prejudice Men againft it ; for that the Clergy have abufed their Power in the Church to Tyranny, is an Objection that Worldly Policy hath made againft the Church's being reftored to her due Power, and againft the fetting up her Difcipline: Which Objection, though it hath no force, for that the Clergy having abufed their Authority, is no Reafon why that Authority which is given the Church by Chrift Jefus fhould not be allowed in its right and due Ufe: Yet it would be a Prejudice if the Clergy fhould act out of their Place and Sphere, and bring the force of the Civil Power upon thofe that live not as they would perfwade them. Would it not prefently be enquired, where was their Power in Chrift to do this ? how it belong'd to their Miniftry, and what Right they had to *Lord it over God's Heritage* by the Force of the Secular Power ? It might juftly be faid, they loved to Ufurp and Exercife a Tyrannical Power, when their own having loft its Credit with the World, they fhould out of a defire to be doing and

acting

acting Tyrannically, be the Instruments of bringing the Power of the Civil Magistrate upon those they should seek to reform by meek and gentle methods. I shall therefore say here, that no Blame can justly lie upon the Clergy of the Church of *England* for what this Author insinuates to be a neglect and Remisness in the greatest part of that Body, that is to say, their not assisting and joyning with the new formed Societies for Reformation in this Kingdom by putting the Laws of the Realm in Execution against Publick Wickedness. 'Tis without all doubt that the Clergy are concerned at all times to seek the Reformation of Christian Professors, and especially in such an Age as this, in which Wickedness so much aboundeth: These have Reason to take to Heart the no greater Success of their Endeavours to give a stop thereto, and upon this Account are concern'd to do all that's possible in their Office and Ministry for that purpose. Insomuch, as though not bound to engage in a Work that is Foreign to their Ministry, and which may give Offence and occasion for the Ministry to be blamed, and evil spoken of, they shall be obliged however, to take notice of what this Author has publickly said, and what themselves know to be too true, that the *Discipline of the Church*

Church is lost, which would have proved a Bank against that Flood of Wickedness which has broken in upon us. And as there is reason to think that the decay and loss of the Church's Discipline hath given a great inlet to that Wickedness which hath overflowed all parts of the Church, 'tis to be hoped we shall not always think it sufficient to lament the loss of the Church's Discipline once a Year in the Office for *Ashwednesday,* but shall in good earnest endeavour to restore the Ancient Discipline, and retrieve the Ecclesiastical Power to its Primitive Design. The Obligation upon all Christians to this seems to me so plain, that I cannot see how Men of Conscience can satisfy themselves with complaining of the Iniquity of the Age and wishing for Reformation, without having recourse to this Remedy. Upon the Clergy especially I look the Obligation is so great to restore this necessary part of their Ministry to some effect, that nothing can be more to them that make Conscience of fulfilling their Ministry in all things.

I suppose the vulgar Prejudice against Excommunication, which is the Penalty that Discipline endeth in, to them that submit not, will not be thought an Objection of any weight to hinder the Restoration of Discipline; that is to say, according

cording to the falſe and weak Notion that many have thereof, that Excommunication is a Cenſure that giveth Men to the Devil. It hath been indeed ſaid before, that it is all one with the *Delivering to Satan* ſpoken of by S. *Paul,* and this in a Spiritual ſenſe, as he that is Caſt out of the Church falleth under the Power of Satan ; but the intention of the Church in putting thus in danger, is to warn Men to flee from the wrath to come, to make haſte to get clear from the Power of Satan. This appeareth in the Practice of the Primitive Church, even towards them that were abſolutely ſhut out of it ; for thoſe whoſe Sins were denied the hope of readmiſſion to Reconcilement with the Church, being refuſed Penance, were yet ſent to God with hope of Mercy ; ſo that not only ſuch as were brought to Penance and allowed the ſame, were recovered out of the Snare of the Devil and ſaved by the Diſcipline and Cenſure of the Church; but even that Key which did wholly ſhut out of the Church, did many times let ino Heaven, and was the means of Salvation to thoſe whom with knowlege it excluded from all hopes of Reconcilement with the Church, to make them ſeek with the more ſolicitude and earneſtneſs, Recociliation with God.

There

There is one Thing, which I forefee may be faid, and framed into fomewhat of an Argument againft what I have been urging concerning a neceffity of Reftoring the Church's Difcipline, which therefore I muft fay fomething to. It is this, That Difcipline is not of the fubftance of Chriftianity but only Minifterial thereunto, that therefore as 'tis in the Power of the Church to alter the way of Exercifing it, and vary the Circumftances thereof as fhall be expedient, fo it is in its Power to abate the ftrictnefs of Difcipline, and even lay afide the ufe of it, if in the Judgment of the Church, the Intreft of Chriftianity fhall fo require. That this was done by the Primitive Church, when in feveral Cafes the ftrictnefs of Difcipline was remitted, and the Communion of the Church granted to Multitudes together without any Penance, to quiet Faction in the Church, or put an end to Schifm, and fometimes only for fake of the great number of Offenders, who, 'twas fuppofed would not fubmit to the Rules of Difcipline. That therefore the prefent Church may, in fo broken and divided a State thereof as now it is in, remit the ftrictnefs of Difcipline for the fake of Unity, wherein it muft be owned the Intreft of Chriftian Religion greatly confifteth ; yea, may

without

without blame in the present diforderly State of Things, when the greater part of Chriftian Profeffors are fo Lewd and Diffolute as to defpife the Power of the Church and flight its Miniftry, even be content to lay afide that Difcipline which is not practicable to be kept up; which being flighted and defpifed by the greater part of Chriftian Profeffors, there is no likelihood any great good can come of it to the Chriftian Religion. To which I anfwer, That indeed the Method of Difcipline has not been always the fame in the Church, and that it is in the Power of the Church to make Alterations therein, taking that Order concerning it, which may be thought to make it moft ferviceable to Chriftianity: Neverthelefs, it cannot be in the Power of the Church to lay the Difcipline of Chrift afide, nor yet to let it fall. The Power of Ordering its Miniftry fo as to make it moft ferviceable and effectual to the purpofes of its Inftitution, is a Right that cannot but belong to the Church, and is of Duty employed by it, is the fulfilling of its Miniftry: But to recede from, or lay afide any part of its Miniftry cannot poffibly be in the Church's Power, becaufe the Church is fubject to Chrift, and bound always to have regard to his Inftitutions; is unfaithful to its

Truft,

Truſt, when it does not take heed to the Miniſtry it is charged with, and which it hath received of the Lord, to fulfil it. And as for what the Primitive Church did in remitting Diſcipline, and abating the ſtrictneſs thereof in ſome particular Caſes, we do not find it was done, but only when there was an urgent neceſſity forcing thereunto, for the avoiding ſome great Miſchief, as when there was fear of Schiſm, or Faction, or ſome Mutiny againſt the Church's Authority from the multitude of Offenders. Beſides, the Church, when it thus condeſcended to abate the ſtrictneſs of its Penance, and give admiſſion to its Communion without it, could not reaſonably be underſtood to intend by the grant of its Communion to warrant forgiveneſs of Sins to thoſe whom ſhe ſo received; any further than that diſpoſition of Mind, which the Parties themſelves knew that they returned with, might warrant it. For it being evident that the Church waved the Rule by which it was wont, and according to which in the due and Regular Exerciſe of its Miniſtry, it ought to proceed; the Charge of making good that diſpoſition which qualifieth before God for the Communion of the Church, did in that reſpect devolve upon the Conſcience of them that impoſed the Neceſſity

ceffity upon the Church to wave its wholfome Rules of Difcipline.. Moreover, though the Primitive Church in particular cafes of neceffity did this to preferve the Being of the Church, which is ever of more moment than the Difcipline thereof; yet afterwards the ftrictnefs of its Difcipline was in all refpects reftored and acted to its proper Ends. So that the Primitive Church never thought it felf to have Power to lay afide the Ordinance of Chrift; but on the contrary, that as the Laws of our Lord and his Apoftles were always an acknowledged Rule to the Church for its Government, fo the Difcipline of their appointment muft be brought to effect by the Church at all times. An exception to a Rule is always looked on as a confirmation of the Rule in all cafes not excepted. Therefore the Primitive Church, keeping always a ftrict Difcipline, and not abating thereof in any cafe, till fatisfied of the Sinners Repentance, but only in a few cafes that were extraordinary, wherein there was a fort of Force and Neceffity upon the Church to do otherwife; Thefe extraordinary cafes can never be pleaded for a ground of Power in the prefent Church to lay afide or let fall the Difcipline which the Church ever ftood charged to adminifter for the Intreft of Chriftianity;

ty ; but rather as they were Extraordinary, there is the greater reason thence to
conclude, that the present Church cannot
be at Liberty to depart from the Example
of the Primitive Church in this particular,
but is more strictly bound to have regard
to that Discipline which is of the appointment, of our Blessed Lord and his Apostles,
and which the Primitive Church we must
suppose thought it self obliged to observe,
for that it did observe it always with great
strictness, preserving by strict Canons
even a Severity of Discipline for several
Ages.   As therefore it is a great mistake
to think that the example of the Primitive
Church, which abated of the strictness of
Discipline in some extraordinary Cases,
will justify our present Remissness in it ;
so I fear it will be found upon examinati-
on, that the common Plea for this Remissness, which is, the broken and divided State
of the Church though it hath too much in
it to the Prejudice of the Christian Religion, hath very little in it to excuse those
that are intrusted by the Church with the
Ministry of its Discipline, for not doing
and discharging their Duty in the Ministration thereof.   For though I will not say
positively and absolutely that the bringing
a few Souls by this Discipline to Repen-
S tance

tance and to the Practice of Piety and Virtue, is of greater service to God and to the Christian Religion, than the gaining of hundreds that are vicious to the side of the established Church, and to a Profession of Communion with it; because the gaining of them to that Communion may be a means of their being gained over afterwards to true Christianity and to the Practice thereof; yet supposing them to continue vicious in the Communion of the Church, this must be said and allowed, though those Hundreds were Thousands. And our having had too long and great Experience, that the Number of true Christians hath not increased among us, how much soever the Number of Proselytes to the Party of the Church may, should make those, methinks, who have the care of the Church upon them and the Charge of its Ministry, concerned and solicitous to employ and exercise their Ministry to the utmost of their Ability for the making those good Christians that are already within the Church, as well as for making Proselytes to it: The one being little to the purpose of men's Salvation, while there is no care taken of the other, or indeed not a due Care. I take it also to be a vain fear, that the Restoring of Discipline in the
Church

The Church of England's *Wish.*

Church would leſſen its Intereſt in the Kingdom, or give to the Schiſms that are on foot an advantage as to number; for it will not be denied I preſume, that Schiſmaticks have taken advantage from the Remiſsneſs of our Diſcipline, or from that at leaſt which is the conſequence of that Remiſsneſs, the ſcandalous Lives of Profeſſors among us, to draw off many well meaning Chriſtians from the preſent eſtabliſhed Church : And it is reaſonable to think that when it ſhall be ſeen that the Miniſtry of the Church and the Diſcipline thereof are exerciſed and acted rightly and zealouſly to the known ends of their Appointment by Chriſt Jeſus , namely, the Converſion of Sinners to Repentance, the Edification of them that do believe, and the Inſtruction and Conduct of them in Righteouſneſs and Godlineſs ; thoſe well meaning Chriſtians, now miſled, may be then brought back into the Church, with many more who are Humble and Peaceable and Pious. When alſo the Lives of Chriſtians who make up the Church ſhall become more Exemplary for Piety and Goodneſs, and it ſhall be viſible that the Diſcipline of the Church contributeth chiefly to their being ſo ; it cannot but be thought that ſuch an Exemplary Converſation

S 2

fation fhould prevail as much or more than any other means what foever to bring Profelytes out of the world to Chriftianity, and to bring thofe that incline to profefs Chriftianity, willingly to profefs it in that Church where the Power and Purity of Religion is feen to be preferved by a Godly Difcipline. Befides, it feems to be agreed by the different Parties in Religion among us, that bad Men are a *Scandal* to the beft Religion, and that they cannot if they continue fo, be faved in any. If therefore Schifmaticks fhould be forward to receive them that fhall be rejected by the Difcipline of the Church, or that may go off from it, becaufe of Difciplines being reftored in it ; I do not fee that the Church has any need at all to envy them the Credit or any other advantage that they are likely to gain by it ; much lefs can I think this a fufficient Reafon for the Church to let its Difcipline fall, which may be exercifed to as great and as full effect, notwithftanding the opportunity that Refractory Sinners may have to go off to Schifmaticks, and even alfo notwithftanding their receiving them, as if there were no Schifm in the Church, nor no Schifmatical Affembly ; that is to fay, before God it may be exercifed to as great and as full effect as if

none

none of thofe things were ; becaufe with him it availeth nothing for a man to profefs Chriftianity in any Society, not being a Chriftian in his Life and Converfation ; alfo before God a Vicious Profeffor departing and going off from the Church, becaufe he will not be Subject to the Difcipline, thereof that would reclaim him from his wickednefs, is difobedient and felf-condemned and the greater Sinner : and though Schifmaticks may pretend, receiving fuch among them, to receive or admit them into the Church of God, or allowing them their Communion to affure their Hopes towards Salvation by the Sacraments of God's Church which they have no Right to Adminifter ; neverthelefs the Church has reafon to declare her Judgment concerning all fuch Pretences, that She efteems them to be, what they really are as to God, even Nullities, void Acts that will deceive and betray thofe Souls in their hopes that depend on them : Void they muft certainly be, as Adminiftred to thofe, whom the Church fhall reject as not qualified before God for Communion with the Church. For tho' it fhould be fuppofed that God of his Goodnefs in compaffion to the ignorance and infirmities of Men, would make good

the

the Acts of men taking upon them to Administer the Sacraments of his Church without a due Authority, when their Integrity before him is such as renders them Innocent in their mistakes ; it is not to be supposed that any of their Acts shall by him be ratified to void the effect of his own Ordinances, and where what they do is with wilful design to void the same ; as the going off of Sinners from the Church to be at their Liberty to live Licentiously, and the receiving of such by any separate Assembly, if they be or shall be received by any, to their Communion in the Offices of God's Service, can be no other than wilful design in both, to Prejudice the Church of God and the effect of the Ministry thereof. I see therefore no reason why the Church should let fall its Discipline on this account ; nor indeed why it should not be resolute in Ministring Discipline, notwithstanding this, believing that as God is able so he will bring to effect his own Ordinance, and make the Ministry of his Church powerful over Wickedness, wheresoever it may seek or find shelter, within or without the Church. Neither may those that stand Charged with the Ministry of the Church hold themselves excused in laying aside or letting fall this

Disci-

Difcipline, for that the greater part of Chriftians are grown fo Lewd and Diffolute as to flight the Authority and defpife the Power of the Church in this particular ; thofe being concerned to *fee that no man defpife them nor their Power in Chrift ; to ufe fharpnefs according to the Power they have received of the Lord for Edification* and the Government of the Church in Godlinefs. It is requifite I allow that there be Prudence ufed in the management of this Power ; it muft alfo be owned, that Prudence directing its management maketh it more ferviceable to Chriftian Purpofes., though its efficacy to thofe ends be from God. This is that which beareth out the Primitive Church in waving the Rules. of its Difcipline , when the Power of the Church was in danger otherwife of being defpifed ; its aim therein being to bring thofe that then ftood againft the Church, under the Government of the Church, and under the Controul of its Difcipline for the future, which Aim was alfo compaffed thereby. The cafe is altogether different where there can be no fuch, or no profpect at leaft of compaffing any fuch Aim ; but if the Difcipline of the Church be laid afide or let fall, it can be with no other Hope or Profpect, than that it muft

be

be let fall for altogether. Now whether
the Church can anſwer it to God, that
She recede from and give up her Power
and Miniſtry, for this that Wicked men
deſpiſe her Power and hold her Miniſtry
in the laſt Contempt, is the Queſtion in
thisCaſe. And I do not believe that anyman's
Conſcience will allow him to think the
Truſt of the Church well diſcharg'd to God,
that ſhall recede from or give up any part
of her Miniſtry or any Powers belonging
to the ſame, for this Reaſon that Wickedneſs exalteth its ſelf againſt her Miniſtry
and ſeeketh to render her Power contemptible. This ought rather to awaken the
Church to make full Proof of its Miniſtry, to exert all the Powers that Chriſt
hath given her to the full, ſo to make appear
that her Aims are not Carnal but Spiritual,
mighty through God to put a ſtop to the
prevailing Power of Wickedneſs. Such
therefore of them that are intruſted with
the Miniſtry of the Church, as are for
conſulting Human Prudence in theſe Circumſtances, and acting their Miniſtry according to worldly Policy, I fear too little
conſult their own Obligations to God and
his Church and the diſcharge thereof with
a good Conſcience. Prudence may and
ought to be uſed at all times, eſpecially

in

The Church of England's *Wish.*

in difficult Circumstances, to direct our
Miniftry to the beft Service and Effect :
But we ought not to fuffer worldly Policy
to raife a Difpute, Whether our Miniftry
fhould be employed or not, to the full
purpofe intended by Chrift. A neceffity
is laid on us to fulfil our Miniftry and
leave the Iffue and Effect to God, who to
fhew that his work dependeth not on man,
hath given it a fuccefs in former time beyond what Human Wifdom could forefee;
and is able ftill to give fuccefs and make his
Work to profper in the hands of his Minifters, even to make that Miniftry of his
Church powerful , which the Infolent
Wickednefs of this Time defpifeth as
weak and contemptible.

C H A P.

C H A P. IX.

IT muſt not be expected from me to ſay now in the Cloſe of this Diſcourſe, what Things are neceſſary to retrieve Diſcipline to its Primitive State and Uſe in the Church. This our Governours are to conſult and account for. The Thing I ſhall take upon me to ſay, is, That an Attempt of this nature ought to be made. Not but that it muſt be ſaid alſo for the Honour of the firſt Reformers of our Church, and of the Reformation in it; That as our Reformation hath been of the greateſt Service to Chriſtianity, in removing thoſe groſs and vile Abuſes that were crept into the Diſcipline of the Church in times of Popery (which not only had perverted it from the uſe it ought to have in the Church of Chriſt, but ſo changed it, that inſtead of being a means to reform, it became the occaſion of a farther Corruption in the Lives and Manners of Chriſtians): So our Church cometh conſiderably nearer to the Apoſtolical Inſtitution in her Diſcipline than moſt others; as

hav-

having retained the ufe of Excommunication, and fome ufe alfo of Penance,
having a Canon that Notorious Offenders
be not admitted to the Communion, and
a particular Order to Parochial Minifters
to refufe fuch. Neverthelefs the Church
has owned that there is a great Defect in
her Difcipline, in that fhe could not reftore Publick Penance, and lamenteth that
fhe could not bring about her Aim in this
for a full Reformation. This we may fuppofe would not have been mentioned, but
with hope that in future time there would
be an Endeavour and might be an Opportunity for that to be compaffed (which
then could not be brought to pafs) for
the Intereft of Religion and the Church of
God. 'Tis not however for private Perfons to make any attempt towards fo good
a Purpofe, any farther than by their
Prayers, that God would put it into the
Hearts of thofe to whom he has committed
the Care and Government of his Church,
to confider of means by which the Difcipline of Chrift may be reftored in his
Church, and the Authority and Power
of the Church retrieved for the exercife
of it to the ends of Religion and Reformation: And that God would pleafe to
infpire them with Godly Zeal and Chriftian

ſtian Courage to uſe all proper and juſt Endeavours in ſo good a work.

What I may ſpeak more freely in, as I hope, without Offence on the part of others, ſo without fear of giving it, or having it taken on my own, is this. That there is a very great and unexcuſable fault, that the Diſcipline which the preſent Church of *England* hath Received, and Eſtabliſhed by its Rules and Canons, and Charged upon thoſe that act in its Miniſtry, is not executed to its due Purpoſe and End in the Church of God. Whether this be chargeable on thoſe that act in the Miniſtry, or on them that perhaps not diſown, but ſlight and deſpiſe the Power of the Miniſtry, and will not be ſubject to wholſom Diſcipline, or on both; I ſay, notwithſtanding that it would be hard to fix the blame of this ſolely on the Miniſtry, both Miniſters and People being in fault, both Corrupted together, and alike; nevertheleſs it more eſpecially concerneth all who have any part in the Miniſtry of this Church, to ſee the Diſcipline of the Church be brought to ſome better effect than it is at preſent, and that thoſe Abuſes, Corruptions, and Defects that are but too viſible in the Miniſtration thereof, (and are the occaſion that for the moſt part it

is

is fet afide; or where ufed, not to the purpofe it fhould be in the Church of Chrift,
but in a manner that giveth Offence to good
Chriftians, and Advantage to thofe that
are otherwife to Reproach and Contemn
the Difcipline it felf, together with them
that act therein) be removed, and fuch
Remedy found, fuch Courfe taken that
the Difcipline of the Church may be Executed with Authority and become effectual
to Chriftian Purpofes. I will take the liberty therefore here to 'fay, that it is a
fault of the Clergy in general, that there
is not that done which is in our Power to
do, not indeed that which by the Eftablifhed Rules of our Church we are obliged to do for the making the Difcipline
thereof of fome effect, to put a Reftraint on
the Loofenefs and great Corruption of the
Age. It is our fault that we do not make
ufe of that Authority and Power which
we have, and may be fupported in from
the Laws of the Land as well as of the
Church ; that I mean, of debarring and
keeping back Notorious Evil Livers from
the Sacrament of the Lord's Supper, and
fuch as are perceived to live in Malice and
Hatred, which the *Rubrick* impowers us
to do, and ftrictly enjoyns to be done.
And the Reverend Bifhops of our Church

to

Rubrick in the Order for admi- niftration of the Lord's Sup- per.

to whom all Curats are to give notice of those whom they so repel, finding, I believe, very few Notices of this kind sent them, have but too much Reason to think that little or nothing of this kind is done, and consequently to require an account of it, and give Charge to their Clergy concerning it; representing the Duty incumbent on them, as they are entrusted with the Ministration of the Sacraments of Christ's Church, and the encrease of Wickedness among Christian Professors through their Remisness and Neglect of Duty in this particular. I shall also desire Leave to say, That 'tis incumbent on the Reverend Bishops of our Church and all others, acting with Authority in the jurisdiction thereof, to make their Visitations to the purpose and effect they were designed in the Church of Christ, the Reformation of the Church and all its Members. 'Tis but too visible to all the World that Visitations have not their wished effect to the ends of Reformation. It must not be said that the whole fault lies in them that have the Government of the Church, that these, from partial regards, from some or other weak and Carnal Considerations are defective in their Duty. Something of this may be, and this may be in part the cause that
Discipline

Difcipline is Adminiftred in no better a manner, and to little purpofe. But there is a fault in Churchwardens, that they have not a ferious regard to their Oath, for making due Prefentations; that whereas the abounding of Iniquity and Licentioufnefs in all Places fhould make them, if they have any Confcience, or the leaft concern for Religion and Chriftianity, take care that the fcandaloufly Wicked of all forts be brought to an account for their Lewd, Unchriftian Living; they are content neverthelefs to overlook and pafs by notorious Wickedneffes, as though they had taken no Truft upon them by their Office, on behalf of the Church of God. There is a fault likewife in Parochial Minifters, that whereas by the Canon they may, and ought to prefent, as they have the higheft Obligations to fupprefs Iniquity, they neverthelefs feldom do any thing of this nature. There is reafon to think however, that thefe would do more in Affiftance of their Bifhops in this Work, if it appeared that our Epifcopal Vifitations could be made with fome effect towards that purpofe, and if there were a Reform made in the fubordinate Officers and Minifters in our Ecclefiaftical Courts, who at prefent, as all the World fees, Manage but very

ill

ill the Power of the Church, converting it chiefly to their own Advantage, with little or no regard to the Ends of Religion; infomuch that the ftrictnefs of Difcipline is wholly abated, the Exercife of that which is Corrupted, the Proceedings againft Offenders, Partial and Dilatory, and if any Penances are enjoyned, 'tis with almoft no Refpect to true Repentance, nor is much Confideration of that had in the Relaxation of fuch Cenfures: So many Subterfuges and Evafions are alfo found almoft in every Cafe, that the good Rules of Difcipline feldom take place. If it be in the Power of the Bifhops of our Church to Redrefs thefe Evils, as in fome meafure doubtlefs it may, it muft certainly be incumbent on them to take fome effectual Courfe therein; if it be not in their Power, for that the Law of the Land may have given an Eftablifhment to fome of thefe Officers independent of the Bifhop; there ought to be a Reprefentation made to the Supreme Power of the Kingdom, how much the Church of Chrift Suffers by this, that its Difcipline cannot be managed according to proper Rules, as Anciently, by Bifhops, with the affiftance of their Clergy; and that the Authority of our Bifhops is under fuch Reftraint from the Legal Eftabifh-

Establishment of Ecclesiastical Officers, as that it cannot make a Reform of Abuses and Corruptions among them that act even under that Authority. The World has long complained of, and indeed the Church long groaned under very great Disorders in the Management of Ecclesiastical Power, and in the Execution of the Church's Discipline; the which 'tis said, our Bishops have not Power to Remedy, but which the Civil Power giving Protection and Effect to the Authority of our Bishops may most certainly with ease Redress. But it belongs to Superiors to attempt in a proper way that Reform which all good Men wish to see effected. 'Tis not for me therefore to speak particularly of these Disorders that are, unless it be of them that are obvious to every view, and that visibly obstruct the effect of Discipline, and make it liable to Reproach and Contempt.

I will not say with some, that it's a direct Obstruction to its Effect, that Lay-Persons act therein, but something to the contrary; Namely, That the People ever had a Right of being satisfied in the Censures that Passed in the Church though no share in the Authority that judged they should pass. The Ancient Custom was,

T   that

that all Acts of this kind Passed at the
Publick Assemblies; and the Prayers of
the People, or of the Church being one
part of the means, to take away Sin by
the Keys of the Church, the other being
the Humiliation of the Penitent, according to that Order and Measure which the
Bishop and his Presbyters prescribed; this
was a ground for the People to give Suf-
frage to the Passing of such Censures as
were advised and resolved on first in the
Consistories of the Clergy. But the Body of Christians growing great and Corrupt withal, by the coming of the World
into the Church, the concurrence of
the People to these and other Acts of
the Church was found to breed intolera-
ble Trouble and Disorder, so that the Bishops, with their Clergy, Managed the
Publick Acts of the Church by themselves
or at least with chosen Persons out of the
People, and those few in number, to avoid
Confusion and Faction. Upon the like
ground the present Church may be content
to admit these Lay-Persons that have Offices in our Ecclesiastical Courts to remain,
and to have Satisfaction on behalf of the
People, that the Power of the Church is
not abused by them that bear that Power,
and that the Proceedings of the Bishops
and

and Clergy are according to the Rules of Discipline, and Justifiable before God and his Church. So that these pretend not to any part of the Ecclesiastical Power themselves, nor to have those that are Vested with that Power by Christ Subordinate to them in the Ministration of Discipline, which would be an Abuse that in probability must hinder all the Wished Effects of Discipline, and make it be thought not to be from the Power of Christ, nor to have any Force upon the Conscience; Whilst those that are to Execute it by Power from him are limited therein by them that have themselves nothing of that Power; and may not of themselves act therein according to the Rules of Christ in his Gospel and their own Judgment of these Rules, but are determined to employ that Power which is Spiritual, after the Will of others, that have no Authority from Christ to Judge in such Matters; whose Sentence consequently will not be allowed to have Force upon the Conscience, for that they are not Vested by Christ with any part of that Power of Binding and Loosing, which Christ hath given to his Church, or at least, no more of it than every other Christian has, that has no Authority over his Brother.

I shall here farther take the Liberty to say, that it is an Abuse of Discipline, and such as greatly hindreth the Effect thereof, being one cause that Men have it in little Esteem; that the Censure of Excommucation is Passed many times for matters of no great moment or importance. That for which in Reason this Sentence is to be feared and regarded is this, That the Exclusion from the Church supposeth *an Exclusion* from God's Mercy and Favour; but if the Sentence that Cuts off from the Church be for a cause that cannot in Reason be thought to cut off from God's Favour, the Sentence will be thought to be invalid, and the Authority pronouncing it will be denied; it being known that the Sentence of the Church, without sufficient Cause doth not cut off from God's Promises; but that the Forfeiture of these is pre-supposed, before a Censure of that nature ought to Pass. It is true indeed, a Wilful Contempt of the Church's Authority carries virtually in it every other Irregularity, and destroys the respect of that Authority, so that the Ends thereof can no way be attained; and consequently the Church that hath no Temporal Force to make her Authority be received, is under a necessity to employ its Censures

in

in that Cafe, though the matter wherein
her Authority is refufed be not of the
greateft moment. It is a Miftake therefore
generally in the People, that think the
Church Excommunicateth for matters of
no moment, when her Cenfures terminate
in this againft fuch as continue in their
Contempt of her Authority, or in a Re-
fufal of her Judgment in thofe Cafes that
in themfelves may not be of fo much moment; for that it always will be of moment that the Authority of the Church be
in no cafe defpifed. But inafmuch as Vulgar
Chriftians will hardly be brought to underftand this, whofe Prejudices neverthelefs the
Church can't but be concerned at all times
to remove; it would be well, if poffible, to
have all ground, yea, and colour for fuch
Prejudices to be taken away : and in that
refpect better it were that the Authority
of the Church were never interpofed in
fuch Matters as the World is not likely to
acknowledge it, than that it fhould be defpifed, together with the Cenfures that
fhould enforce it upon Men's Confciences
by reafon thereof. The matters in which
the World doth not readily acknowledge
the Church's Power and Authority, are
Civil Rights, and Caufes of a Secular Nature. Though it is true, that in the be-

T 3   ginning,

ginning, Caufes and Controverfies of that nature among Chriftians were decided within
the Church, upon which ground S. *Paul* for-
bids them going to Law in the *Gentile*
Courts, that they might not bring Scandal
upon their Religion by their Contentions.
But when the Civil Powers became Chriftian, the Scandal of going to Law ceafed, and
fo the Right of determining Difputes about
Civil Matters hath reverted from the
Church to the Civil Magiftrate. Thofe
things of this kind that at prefent the
Church's Jurifdiction extendeth to, are
within its Jurifdiction by conceffion of the
Civil Power, continuing the Church in
fome part of that Authority by Favour,
which it had of Right in fuch Matters Anciently, when the Civil Power was not
Chriftian. Now as thefe things more properly belong to the Law of the Land to
determine, and as Confcience doth not
feem to be always concerned in them,
at leaft, not fo much as that every
Body will think that fuch as may refufe
to do Right therein fhall be Excluded the
Kingdom of Heaven, therefore the Church
proceeding to enforce its Sentence in fuch
Matters by Cenfures, which terminate in
Excommunication of thofe that refufe to
obey its determination; the Vulgar prefently

fently are apt to conclude, that the Church
abuſeth its Power in Chriſt, in Excommu-
nicating for little Matters, ſuch as there
is not ſufficient reaſon to think will exclude
from the Kingdom of Heaven ; not confidering that Diſobedience and Contempt of
the Authority of the Church of Chriſt is
always a great Evil : But this being a thing
that few will be brought to confider, the
greater part in this Age being more incli-
nable to keep up Prejudices againſt them
that bear the Power of the Church, upon
undue grounds, than to admit Reaſonable
Confiderations that would remove them ;
therefore I cannot but be of Opinion that
it were better the Juriſdiction of the
Church were not concerned with ſuch
Matters, or at leaſt, that the Chriſtian
Magiſtrate, that alloweth the Church
ſuch Juriſdiction, would enforce the Sentence of the Church in ſuch Cafes by
Law and Civil Puniſhment, that the
Church might not be neceſſitated to
make uſe of Eccleſiaſtical Cenſures in
caſes where they are likely to be Deſpiſed, and the Authority of the Church
held as Contemptible.

I ſhall here moreover take Leave to ſay,
that its a Corruption of Diſcipline ; if
there be any Partiality either to Sins, or

Per-

Persons: If there be any Partiality as
to Sins, some Censured, and others not;
for it is not to be thought that Christ, in
Setling such a Power and Order as this
in his Church, should intend otherwise
but that it should take Cognizance of
all Sins Notorious and Heinous, that
none escape Uncensured: Or if there be
any Partiality or Respect of Persons, if
a Great Man be let alone in his *Licentiousness,* because he has either Power
or Money; or indeed, if other *Sinners*
are let alone and passed by, because they
are too little, and no Profit to be made
of them. There is also a Defect, and it
will ever be a Reflection upon the Dici-
pline of the Church, if it appear not
that the main aim of those that are any
way concerned in the Ministration of
Discipline, is indeed that which the Discipline was Instituted for, namely, The
due Government of Christ's Church in
Piety and Godliness, and the Reformation of whatsoever should be Amiss
therein. I would not be taken to suggest that it is not Reasonable that those
that Attend upon any Part of the Ministry should not Live upon their Office,
but I would have all such make it appear, that they have in view chiefly the
Ser-

Service and Benefit of God's Church and People, Reformation, and not their own Gain or Secular Intrest.

Let me have Leave also here to say, that its a Fault and a Corruption of Discipline to admit, or accept Commutations for Penance; For though Acts of Charity are the Tokens of a Penitent Mind, and avail much towards the obtaining God's Favour and Mercy, according to that which the Apostle has said of *Charity,* that it *covereth a Multitude of Sins*; Yet a forced Gift to the Poor, for certain can be of no Avail. The Apostle supposes, a Man may give all his Goods to the Poor, and yet not have Charity. An Offender may give to avoid Censure, or rather, Secular Inconveniences from it; but shall that be esteemed Charity, or shall it be presumed a Token and Sign of Repentance? Yea, he may give Voluntarily, and yet continue in his Sins; and shall Charity be thought an Expiation for Sins wilfully continued in? or indeed, a Satisfaction to God's Church, as to the taking off Ecclesiastical Censures pass'd on such, when their Amendment other ways appears not? It withal brings an Evil Report even on the Discipline it self, as

well

well as on them that Minister it. I hope, with us there is no such thing as putting up Commutation-Summs, but 'tis well known such things have been Objected, as though the Ministers of Discipline put themselves in place of the Poor. It were therefore questionless much better if Commutations were never medled with; it would remove all Scandal, and prevent false Reports, and be never the worse for the Poor. For if the Discipline of the Church can bring once Sinners to be truly Penitent, they will be of themselves disposed to do Voluntary Acts of Charity.

These Defects and Abuses, and whatsoever others there are that may hinder in any respect the wished Effects in Discipline, all who have any hand, or part in the Ministry are concerned, if possible, to remove and remedy. And so valuable would the Effects of Discipline be, duly Exercised and Administred, to the Church of God and the Intrest of our common Christianity, that I shall say without fear of Contradiction, that it would be the Glory of our Reformation to bring it to be of Effect, as it is now our Reproach, that we have suffered the Discipline of Chrift's Church to be laid aside fide, and rejected in the most essential parts of it, and to be so Corrupted in what remains thereof with us, that the same is in a manner of no Effect or Advantage to the Church of God.

But if our Sins are still too Powerful to suffer the due and right course of Ecclesiastical Discipline to take place among us as it ought, let me advertise all good Christians of a private Benefit and Advantage which every Man may make to himself from what has appeared in this Discourse, of the Nature and Intent of Discipline, while those who are concerned to bring it to Effect do it not, or labour to do it, but without Success. If this Discipline cannot be brought to a due Effect throughout the Church, i. e. to be Exercised for its true Purposes, and Submitted to for its true End; nevertheless, every Man may learn from what this Discipline was, and from what it ought to be, something that concerneth the state of his own Soul, and how to supply in some measure to himself the want of the due Effect of this Ordinance of Christ, which is become defective through the Wickedness of Men. Every one must be sensible, from what hath been here before said of the nature of Discipline, and its

Practice

Practice in the Primitive Church; that whofoever was Admitted into the Church of Chrift, was Admitted upon his Engagement to live Chriftianly, this being indeed the Refolution that entitled to the Mercy of God in Chrift Jefus upon the Terms of the Gofpel; that whofoever failed of performing and making good this his Undertaking, forfeited thereby all Right to the Bleffings of the Covenant, and was therefore, by them that had the Overfight and Care of the Church of God to be called to Account, to be Rebuked and Cenfured, and if found Obftinate in Wickednefs, to be Cut off from the Church of God; that fuch an one might thereby be made fenfible that his Sins had cut him off from the hope of Salvation; whereof this Advantage every Man may, and it is to be hoped, will make for himfelf, to wit, conclude, and judge aright concerning the ftate of his own Soul, that is to fay, That if his own Heart Condemn him of Sins inconfiftent with Chriftianity, he reckon that God will much more Condemn him; and betake himfelf therefore immediately to Reform every Evil Practice, not daring to prefume on God's Mercy and Favour whilft he lives in Sins unrepented,

within

The Church of England's Wish.

within the Bosom of a Church, wherein the Discipline of Christ not having place, his Admission to the Sacraments cannot be to him a sufficient Presumption of a sure Interest in the Benefits of Christ; but concluding that though he be not cut off from the Society of God's Church, yet, his sins unrepented, justly cut off his hopes of God's Favour, and will utterly Exclude him from his Heavenly Kingdom; if he be not so true to the Interest of his Soul, as henceforth to become a True Penitent.

F I N I S.

Books Printed for W. Rogers.

Bishop of *Bath* and *Wells* his Commissary on the Pentateuch, 2*d.* Vol. 8*vo.*

———— A Demonstration of the *Messias*, 2*d.* and 3*d.* Vol 8*vo.*

Dr. *Sherlock's* Practical Discourse concerning Death. 12*th.* Edition, 8*vo.*

———— Practical Discourse concerning Judgment, 5*th.* Edition 8*vo.*

———— Discourse concerning Divine Providence. 3*d.* Edition 8*vo.*

———— Practical Discourse of Religious Assemblies, 4*th.* Edition, 8*vo.*

———— Sermons Preached upon several Occasions, 2*d.* Edit. 8*vo.*

———— Sermon before the King at *Hampton-Court*, June 1. 1691. 4*to.*

———— *Concio ad Sanctam Synodum ab Archiepiscopo, Episcopis & Clero Provinciae Cantuariensis Celebratam, Habita in Ecclesia Cathedrali S. Pauli London. December* 3*d.* A. D. 1701.

———— Exhortation to the Redeemed Slaves of *Machaness.* 8*vo.* price 3*d.*

———— Vindication of the Doctrine of the Trinity. 3*d.* Edition, 4*to.*

———— Present State of the *Socinian* Controversie, and the Doctrine of the Catholick Fathers concerning a Trinity in Unity. 4*to.*

Dr. *Claget's* Sermons upon several Occasions, with his Paraphrase on the 6*th.* of *St. John,* in Two Vol. 8*vo.*

Mr. *Hodges's* Treatise of the Lawfulness of the Marriage of the Clergy, 8*vo.*

Erasmus's Weapon for a Christian Soldier, 12*o.*

Mr. *Park's* New and Easie Method to Sing by Book, 8*vo.*

———— The Art of Spelling, 2*d.* Edit. 8*vo.*

Bulstrode's Reports. in Three Parts. 2*d.* Edit. *Fol.*

Bendloe and *Dallison's* Reports, Published by M. *Rowe,* 1689. *Fol.*

A Discourse of the Growth of *England* in Trade since the Reformation. *Fol.*

Mr. *Lortie's* Practical Discourse concerning Repentance, 12*o.*

Mr. *Ellis's* Necessity of Serious Consideration and Speedy Repentance. 2*d.* Edition, 8*vo.*

———— Folly of Atheism Demonstrated to the Capacity of the most Unlearned Reader, 8*vo.*

———— Summ of Christianity, 3*d.* Edit. 8*vo.* price 3*d.*

———— Scripture Catechism. Second Edition, 8*vo.* price 3*d.*

Mr.

Books Printed for W. Rogers.

Mr. *Wilson*'s Difcourfe of Religion, fhewing its Truth and Reality, or the fuitablenefs of Religion to Humane Nature, 8*vo*.

——Difcourfe of the Refurrection, fhewing the Import and Certainty of it, 8*vo*.

Mr. *Dreyden*'s Tranflation of C. A. du *Frefnoy*'s Art of Painting, with Remarks: Together with an Original Preface, containing a Parallel betwixt Painting and Poetry, as alfo an Account of the moft Eminent Painters, 4*to*.

Mr. *Jenks*'s Prayers and Offices of Devotions for Families, and particular Perfons, on moft Occafions, the 2d. Edition 12°.

——Submiffion to the Righteoufnefs of God, 8*vo*.

——Bell Rung to Prayers, 12°.

——Meditations, with fhort Prayers annexed, in Ten Decades, upon vaiious Subjects, 12°.

The Liberty of Prayer Afferted, and Guarded from Licentioufnefs, by a Minifter of the Church of *England*, 8*vo*.

Sr. *John Davies*, of the Immortality of the Soul, 8*vo*.

Scala Sancta, or the Exaltation of the Soul, 8*vo*.

Dr. *Pelling*'s Practical Difcourfe concerning Holinefs, 8*vo*.

—— Difcourfe concerning the Exiftence of God.

Mr. *Tyrrel*'s General Hiftory of *England*, both Ecclefiaftical and Civil, from the Earlieft Account of Time, to the Reign of King *William* I. commonly called the Conquerer. Vol. I. *Folio*.

——General Hiftory of *England*, both Ecclefiaftical and Civil, from the beginning of the Reign of King *William* I. to the end of the Reign of King *Henry* III. Vol. II.

Mr. *Wake*'s Difcourfe againft Tithe-Stealing. 4*to*.

The New Danger of Presbytery, &c. 4*to*.

A 558460 ᴰᵁᴾᴸ

CPSIA information can be obtained
at www.ICGtesting.com
Printed in the USA
BVHW041431150819
555988BV00011B/581/P

9 781406 902051